THE MILITARY AND DEMOCRACY IN INDONESIA

Challenges, Politics, and Power

Angel Rabasa ◆ **John Haseman**

Supported by the
Smith Richardson Foundation

RAND

National Security Research Division

The research described in this report was sponsored by the Smith Richardson Foundation. The research was conducted through the International Security and Defense Policy Center (ISDPC) of RAND's National Security Research Division (NSRD).

Library of Congress Cataloging-in-Publication Data

Rabasa, Angel.
    The military and democracy in Indonesia : challenges, politics, and power /
Angel Rabasa, John Haseman.
      p. cm.
    "MR-1599-SRF."
    Includes bibliographical references.
    ISBN 0-8330-3219-4 (alk. paper)
    1. Civil-military relations—Indonesia. 2. Indonesia—Politics and government—
20th century. 3. Indonesia—Armed Forces—Reorganization. 4. Indonesia—Armed
Forces—Political activity. 5. United States—Military relations—Indonesia. 6.
Indonesia—Military relations—United States. I. Haseman, John B. II.Title.

JQ766.C58 R33 2002
322'.5'09598—dc21

                                      2002011612

RAND is a nonprofit institution that helps improve policy and decisionmaking through research and analysis. RAND® is a registered trademark. RAND's publications do not necessarily reflect the opinions or policies of its research sponsors.

Published 2002 by RAND
1700 Main Street, P.O. Box 2138, Santa Monica, CA 90407-2138
1200 South Hayes Street, Arlington, VA 22202-5050
201 North Craig Street, Suite 202, Pittsburgh, PA 15213-1516
RAND URL: http://www.rand.org/
To order RAND documents or to obtain additional information,
contact Distribution Services: Telephone: (310) 451-7002;
Fax: (310) 451-6915; Email: order@rand.org

Indonesia, the world's fourth most populous country and the largest one with a Muslim majority, is undergoing a systemic political transition that could lead to a variety of outcomes, including democratic consolidation, a return to authoritarianism, the rise of radical Islam, or even disintegration. The Indonesian military is one of the few institutions that cuts across the divides of Indonesian society and will play a critical role in determining the country's future evolution. But the military, like other Indonesian institutions, is itself undergoing profound change. Which path Indonesia and its armed forces will follow remains unclear.

This study examines the role of the military in Indonesian politics and society since the fall of Indonesian president Suharto in 1998. The key issues under analysis are: (1) What role will the military play in influencing Indonesia's political evolution—Will it be a constructive force supporting democratic processes or will it opt for authoritarian solutions? (2) What are realistic goals for further progress on military reform? (3) How can the United States engage the Indonesian military most effectively to help bring about positive change?

The research issues of this study are central to the strategic interests of the United States in Asia and are directly related to the Smith Richardson Foundation's view that the United States continues to face the challenge of enhancing international order and advancing U.S. interests and values abroad. This report should be of value to the national security community and interested members of the general public, especially those with an interest in U.S. relations with Indonesia and U.S. policy toward the Asia-Pacific region. Comments are welcome and may be sent to either the authors or to Ambassador (retired) James Dobbins, director of RAND's International Security and Defense Policy Center, at RAND, 1200 South Hayes Street, Arlington, VA 22202-5050.

This research was funded by a grant from the Smith Richardson Foundation and conducted within the International Security and Defense Policy Center of RAND's National Security Research Division (NSRD). NSRD conducts research and analysis for the Office of the Secretary of Defense, the Joint Staff, the Unified Commands, the defense agencies, the Department of the Navy, the U.S. intelligence community, allied foreign governments, and foundations.

CONTENTS

FIGURES

TABLES

Indonesia's future is highly uncertain. The collapse of former president Suharto's authoritarian "New Order" in 1998 made way for a political process that has led Indonesia on a path toward democracy, a development that is pregnant with possibilities. However, Indonesia's fragile democratic experiment is threatened by multiple crises. Despite the uncertainty surrounding Indonesia's future, some conditions can be expected to hold for the next several years. The country's recovering economy will remain fragile and vulnerable to external and internal shocks. Indonesia's political process will remain under stress. The role of Islam in politics—which goes back to the fundamental question of the nature of the Indonesian state—will continue to be a sensitive and potentially divisive issue. And the military, despite its formal subordination to civilian authority, will continue to play a key role in national security decisionmaking and will be an important influence on the country's political evolution.

The Indonesian military, with its tradition of secular nationalism, is one of the few institutions that cut across the many divides of Indonesian society. And, like all other Indonesian institutions, the military is itself in the process of change. The multiple crises that accompanied the fall of Suharto prompted a reexamination of the military's role. The national military, renamed Tentara Nasional Indonesia (TNI), responded to the pressures for change by reducing its political profile and undertaking a revision of its doctrine. The military also jettisoned the doctrine of "dual function" (*dwifungsi*) that gave it an institutionalized role in politics, acquiesced in the reduction and eventual elimination of its corporate representation in the country's legislative bodies, and began to reorient its mission from internal security to external defense. Indonesia began to take the first steps toward democratic civilian control of the military while, for the first time since the 1950s, civilian ministers have taken the reins of the country's Department of Defense.

There is no doubt that change has already occurred in the TNI and that additional change may still lie in the future, but the adjustments will be difficult and the outcome cannot be certain. The requirements in the new democratic era to adapt, change, and even eliminate missions, organizational structures, and doctrines learned throughout the years have created a stressful environment for military personnel at every level. The majority view in the TNI remains in favor of gradual change within a democratic political framework. However, institutional inertia, lack of competent civilian leadership, and the practical difficulties in implementing strategic change within the armed forces have diminished the momentum of the reforms.

A key question is whether cracks exist in the solid front the TNI strives to present to the world that might destabilize the military institution. The armed forces have maintained their unity and solidarity throughout the twists and turns of the post-Suharto political transition. Despite stresses on the institution, the military appears united. Nevertheless, in Indonesia's new freewheeling political environment, there is intense competition among civilian politicians for supporters within the senior TNI ranks. Senior military officers are torn among loyalty to their seniors in the old military, loyalty to the institution, and loyalty to a new chain of command with inexperienced civilians at the top.

The evolution of the internal security situation could be a critical factor in determining the military's future political orientation. Indonesia is confronting a plethora of security threats from several different directions: armed separatists, radical Islamic organizations and militias, and factions engaged in intercommunal conflict and religious wars in the province. A deteriorating situation and the danger of national disintegration could impel the military to reenter politics or derail the democratic process.

This study postulates six strategic scenarios for Indonesia, each with important implications for the Indonesian military and for U.S.–Indonesian relations:

- **Scenario 1: Democratic Consolidation.** In the best-case scenario, Indonesia continues to develop along a secular, democratic trajectory; makes progress in resolving some of the critical problems in the economy; satisfies demands for provincial autonomy; and continues to make progress on military reform. In this scenario, the United States would be in a strong position to normalize military relations with Indonesia.

- **Scenario 2: Muddling Through.** The second scenario builds on trends that are already evident. Indonesia continues on a democratic path, but Jakarta fails to make headway on economic and military reform, or fails to take meaningful action against terrorist and radical Islamic groups. In this scenario, the United States would still find it in its best interest to strengthen military relations with Indonesia, but advocates of closer military relations may find it difficult to overcome congressional and other opposition.

- **Scenario 3: A Return to Authoritarianism.** A continued inability of the new democratic institutions to deliver stability, competent government, and economic growth could generate a demand for the return of a strong ruler. Several models could develop under this scenario. The United States' ability to engage Indonesia would depend on the specific circumstances of the turn of events there.

- **Scenario 4: Radical Islamic Influence or Control.** A radical Islamic takeover is possible, but should be considered a low-probability scenario at this stage. However, in the view of some, it is only a matter of time before the pattern of political competition in Indonesia opens more space for radical Islam, especially if economic conditions do not improve. It would not be realistic to expect any meaningful U.S. engagement with the Indonesian military in this scenario, and the United States might find it necessary to conduct counterterrorist operations in Indonesia.

- **Scenario 5: Federation.** An exhausted or weakened central government under pressure from the outer regions might permit, or be forced to accept, more wide-ranging autonomy initiatives. This scenario might evolve into a central state that could be inherently unstable.

- **Scenario 6: Territorial Disintegration.** This could be the end stage of some of the downside scenarios we just described. A breakup of Indonesia would have catastrophic consequences for U.S. interests and regional security. U.S. policy would focus on mitigating the consequences of this development.

Cooperation between the United States and the Indonesian military has been intermittent and hindered by tensions over human rights issues and by congressionally mandated sanctions. However, one of the principal sources of tension between the United States and Indonesia—the status of East Timor and human rights violations by Indonesian security forces and military-backed militias in East Timor—has largely dissipated as East Timor achieved its independence and Indonesia cooperated in stabilizing the border, curtailing the activities of pro-Indonesian militias who took refuge in West Timor, and facilitating the return of refugees. What remains to be addressed is whether Indonesia can meet the requirement for accountability by those responsible for the violence in the wake of the 1999 East Timor referendum (see the appendix for a further discussion).

Indonesia's painful progress toward democracy—and the military's support in this process—has created opportunities for a closer relationship between the U.S. and Indonesian militaries. This increased interaction provides the United States with a foundation to help shape the Indonesian military's capability to deal constructively with the challenge of rebuilding civil-military relations based on democratic principles.

GOALS FOR INDONESIAN MILITARY REFORM

In our policy recommendations presented in Chapter Thirteen, we discuss the goals for Indonesian military reform, which address the following areas:

- **The army's territorial structure.** The goal should be to begin the process of dismantling the territorial structure in those areas where the security conditions do not require a continued military role.

- **Civil-military relations.** The TNI should be encouraged and helped to deal constructively with the challenge of building a new model of civil-military relations based on democratic principles. In doing their own part, individuals in the civilian sector need to develop a depth and range of knowledge in defense matters that would make their views respected by the military. Civilians appointed to senior positions in the Indonesian Department (Ministry) of Defense should have the requisite functional expertise.

- **Military business activities.** The long-term goal should be the military's withdrawal from its business activities. However, it is not realistic to expect that the TNI could be funded entirely out of the state budget in the near term. Therefore, for the present, the goal should be to increase transparency and accountability in military-run enterprises.

- **Human rights.** The more thoughtful TNI leaders recognize the importance of improving the military's human rights performance, but lasting change in this area will be cultural and evolutionary and would be most successfully promoted through the use of positive incentives that reinforce trends already underway in Indonesia, rather than through sanctions.

- **Links to rogue groups and Muslim extremists.** Political stabilization and the development of healthy civil-military relations, as well as the demands of military professionalism, will require the Indonesian political leadership and the TNI to take meaningful actions to break these links.

ELEMENTS OF AN EFFECTIVE U.S. ENGAGEMENT STRATEGY

An effective U.S. engagement program should focus on providing the Indonesian military with the doctrines, training, and resources to implement its reform program and to develop the capability to defend the country's unity and territorial integrity.

Restoring International Military Education and Training (IMET) funding for Indonesia is the first priority. Because military training for Indonesia was effectively terminated in 1992, there has been a "lost generation" of Indonesian officers—officers who have not been exposed to U.S. military culture and values and who have no understanding of the importance the U.S. military attaches to civilian leadership, democracy, and respect for human rights. It is no accident that the senior officers who led the Indonesian military reform movement after the fall of Suharto were trained in the United States, but as those officers retire, they are being replaced by others who are more conservative in their outlook and less committed to reform.

An initial IMET package for Indonesia could include nonlethal training; military medical training (for instance, trauma skills courses for troops engaged in field operations); safety training for the air force and navy; legal training, especially in rules of engagement and discipline problems; counterterrorism training; and higher military education.

Indonesian military personnel should be invited to participate in the next Cobra Gold exercise (a large, annual, multilateral exercise involving the United States, Thailand, and Singapore). Indonesian counterterrorist and special forces should also be encouraged to participate in training exchanges with Philippine military units, such as the Scout Rangers, who have already been exposed to U.S. training.

Another part of this engagement strategy would be to provide the assistance needed to prevent any further deterioration of Indonesian military capabilities, particularly in the area of air transport. The reported George W. Bush administration's proposal to help Indonesia with the training and equipping of a dedicated peacemaking unit, if implemented, would be an important contribution to the reestablishment of a climate of peace and security. The United States should also extend support to the Indonesian marine and navy units that have the ability to conduct maritime counterterrorist operations and interdict illegal arms shipments to Aceh and the Moluccas.

The United States can achieve important counterterrorism objectives by providing training and technical support for Indonesia's civilian state intelligence agency Badan Intelijen Negara (BIN), and the military intelligence organization Badan Intelijen Strategis (BAIS). The focus of the assistance program could be on improving technical collection and analytical capabilities.

It is important to realize that there are limits to the ability of the United States to influence a country of 220 million people, a country, moreover, with a history of sensitivity to issues of sovereignty. An excessively intrusive approach would be resented by the Indonesian people and would be exploited by radicals or other forces that are hostile to the United States and the values that it represents. These factors can complicate the task of developing a constructive cooperative relationship between the U.S. and Indonesian governments and militaries, but do not reduce the importance of that relationship.

ACKNOWLEDGMENTS

The authors wish to thank all those who made this study possible. We have many to thank. First of all, we wish to thank the Smith Richardson Foundation for providing the funding that made this publication possible and our project officer, Allan Song, who shepherded the study from proposal to completion. We thank the reviewers of this report, Dr. Adam Schwarz and Colonel (retired) Charles D. McFetridge, a graduate of the Indonesian Army Command and General Staff School and former U.S. defense attaché in Jakarta, for their corrections and suggestions. It goes without saying that any errors that remain are entirely the authors' responsibility.

We also wish to acknowledge the assistance of the U.S. embassies in Jakarta and Singapore, with special thanks to the U.S. Air Force attachés, Colonel Robert Belkowski in Jakarta and Colonel James Tietjen and Captain Steven Howery in Singapore. Our thanks, too, to S. Bram Brotodiningrat and Dan Getz for helping us with the compilation of important materials. Within RAND, this research was conducted under the auspices and with the support of the International Security and Defense Policy Center, directed by Ambassador (retired) James Dobbins. We also thank our editor Nancy DelFavero and our production editor Chris Kelly.

Our most important sources were government and military officials and academics and research institutions in Indonesia, Singapore, and the United States. For their cooperation with this project, we wish to thank Lieutenant General (retired) Susilo Bambang Yudhoyono, coordinating minister for Political and Security Affairs, and his deputies Ambassador Amin Rianom and Major General

Bambang Sutedjo; Lieutenant General (retired) Abdullah M. Hendropriyono, head of the state intelligence agency (BIN) and his principal deputy, Bom Soerjanto; Air Vice Marshal Ian Santoso, director of the military intelligence agency (BAIS) and his staff; Lieutenant General Agus Widjojo, deputy speaker of the People's Consultative Assembly (MPR); Lieutenant General Johny Lumintang, secretary-general of the Department of Defense; Major General Sudrajat, director general for Defense Planning, Department of Defense; Dr. Juwono Sudarsono, Indonesia's first civilian minister of defense since the 1950s; Bambang Harymurti, editor-in-chief of the magazine *Tempo;* Ken Conboy of the Control Risks Group; Derwin Pereira, Indonesia bureau chief of *The Straits Times* of Singapore and author of an excellent series of articles on the TNI; and Dennis Heffernan, publisher of the *Van Zorge Report on Indonesia.*

In the scholarly community, we thank Jusuf Wanandi for his invaluable help, and also Hadi Soesastro, executive director of Jakarta's Centre for Strategic and International Studies (CSIS), Rizal Sukma and other members of the CSIS staff; Indria Samego, director of the postgraduate program at Jayabaya University and author of important works on the Indonesian military; Nurcholish Madjid, Indonesia's foremost Islamic scholar; Bruce Harker, Aceh project director of the Institutional Reform and the Informal Sector Project of the University of Maryland; and so many others who met with us during our visits to Indonesia and shared their knowledge with us.

Some of our most important insights came from discussions with officials and academics in Singapore, particularly the staff of the Institute of Defence and Strategic Studies of the Nanyang Technological University.

The conferences organized by the United States–Indonesia Society were, as always, an invaluable resource in this study. We thank the ambassadors and staff of the embassies of Indonesia and Singapore in Washington for their invaluable assistance with our visits to their countries and their contribution to a dialogue on political dynamics and security issues in Southeast Asia.

ACRONYMS AND DEFINITIONS

ABRI	Angkatan Bersenjata Republik Indonesia (Armed Forces of the Republic of Indonesia)
ADC	Aide-de-camp
ASEAN	Association of Southeast Asian Nations
BAIS	Badan Intelijen Strategis (Strategic Intelligence Service)
BAKIN	Badan Koordinasi Intelijen Negara (State Intelligence Coordinating Board)
BIN	Badan Intelijen Negara (State Intelligence Agency)
Bulog	State Logistics Agency
CSIS	Center for Strategic and International Studies
Dephan	Departemen Pertahanan (Indonesian Department of Defense)
DPR	Dewan Perwakilan Rakyat (People's Representative Council or House of Representatives)
E-IMET	Expanded IMET
FPI	Front Pembela Islam (Islam Defenders Front)
FY	Fiscal year
GAM	Gerakan Aceh Merdeka (Free Aceh Movement)

GDP	Gross domestic product
Golkar	Golongan Karya (Functional Groups)
ICMI	Indonesian Association of Islamic Intellectuals
IMET	International Military Education and Training
INTERFET	International Peacekeeping Force for East Timor
ISEAS	Institute of Southeast Asian Studies (Singapore)
JCET	Joint Combined Exchange and Training
KNIL	Koninklijk Nederlandsch–Indische Leger (Netherlands East Indies Army [Dutch colonial army])
Kodam	Komando Daerah Militer (Military Area Command[s])
Korem	Komando Resor Militer (Military Resor Command[s])
Kodim	Komando Distrik Militer (Military District Command[s])
Ko-Op	Operational Command
Kopassus	Army Special Forces Command
Koramil	Komando Rayon Militer (Military Subdistrict Command[s])
Kostrad	Army Strategic Reserve Command
KMM	Kumpulan Militant Malaysia (Malaysian Militant Group)
Lemhannas	National Resilience Institute
MMI	Majelis Mujahidin Indonesia (Indonesian Mujahidin Council)
MPR	Majelis Permusyawaratan Rakyat (People's Consultative Assembly)
Mubes	Musyawarah Besar (Great Consultation provincial assembly) (Papua)

NCO	Noncommissioned officer
NGO	Nongovernmental organization
OPM	Organisasi Papua Merdeka (Free Papua Organization)
PETA	Pasukan Sukarela Tentara Pembela Tanah Air (Defenders of the Fatherland)
PDI	Partai Demokrasi Indonesia (Indonesian Democratic Party)
PDI-P	Partai Demokrasi Indonesia Perjuangan (Indonesian Democratic Party–Struggle)
PKI	Partai Komunis Indonesia (Indonesian Communist Party)
PNI	Partai Nasional Indonesia (Indonesian National Party)
PPP	Partai Persatuan Pembangunan (United Development Party [Muslim])
PRRI	Pemerintahan Revolusioner Republik Indonesia (Revolutionary Government of the Republic of Indonesia)
PSI	Partai Sosialis Indonesia (Indonesian Socialist Party)
SAIS	School of Advanced International Studies (Washington, D.C.)
Sesko AD	Indonesian Army Command and Staff School
Sesko AL	Indonesian Navy Command and Staff School
Sesko AU	Indonesian Air Force Command and Staff School
Sesko TNI	Joint Senior Service Staff College
TNI	Tentara Nasional Indonesia (Indonesian National Military)
USINDO	United States–Indonesia Society

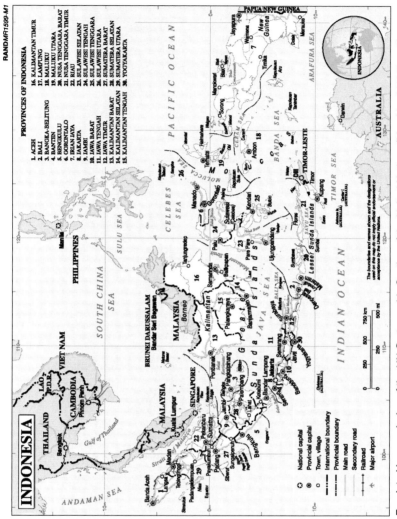

Reprinted by permission of the UN Cartographic Section of the United Nations (Map No. 4110 Rev. 3).

Chapter One

INTRODUCTION

Indonesia has been described as the least known of the world's most important countries. Its importance derives from well-known geopolitical factors. It is the world's fourth most populous country and the largest Muslim-majority country, with a population and a land mass almost as large as those of the rest of Southeast Asia combined, vast natural resources and economic potential, and a strategic location straddling critical sea lanes and straits—all of which makes it the key to Southeast Asia's security. A stable, strong, and democratic Indonesia could resume its leadership role in the Association of Southeast Asian Nations (ASEAN), further regional integration based on democratic principles, contribute to maintaining regional stability, and deter potential Chinese adventurism. Conversely, an unstable or disintegrating Indonesia would make the regional security environment more unpredictable and dangerous, create opportunities for forces seeking to subvert the regional status quo, and generate large-scale humanitarian demands on the international community.

Beyond that, the outcome of Indonesia's democratic experiment could have a major impact in shaping the political evolution of Asia and of the larger Muslim world. If Indonesia's democratic transition holds, it will be the world's third-largest democracy as well as the largest secular democracy in the Muslim world. This transition could have enormously important global consequences. The future of Islam, some argue, will not be decided in its Arab heartland with its authoritarian and intolerant models of governance, but in countries such as Indonesia, where Islam has not jelled into a fundamentalist mold and where democracy remains an attainable prospect.[1]

This not to suggest that the road to democracy and stability in Indonesia will be a smooth one. From the accession of B. J. Habibie to the presidency, after Suharto's 32-year rule ended with his resignation in May 1998, to President Abdurrahman Wahid's removal by the People's Consultative Assembly in July 2001, the country's transition to democracy has been upset by power struggles, riots, terrorist attacks, and ethnically targeted massacres. Megawati Sukarnoputri's succession to the presidency defused the political crisis that preceded President Wahid's removal from power. Nevertheless, the obstacles to democratic consolidation in Indonesia remain formidable. The economic recovery, such as it is, remains fragile and vulnerable to internal and external shocks. At the same time, Indonesia continues to be wracked by localized ethnic and religious conflict and faces serious threats to its unity and territorial integrity.

These challenges to Indonesia's stability were compounded by the September 11 attacks on the United States and their global consequences. In the aftermath of the attacks, the U.S. agenda in Southeast Asia and elsewhere changed in a fundamental way. Before September 11, terrorism in Southeast Asia was a concern, but not a dominant U.S. priority, and the threat of radical Islam was also not fully recognized. September 11 changed that. Now, Southeast Asia is regarded as a major battlefield in the war on terrorism, and terrorist groups are no longer seen as local threats, but as part of larger and more dangerous regional and global networks.

President Megawati was the first leader of a major Muslim country to visit Washington, D.C., after September 11 and express support for the war on terrorism. However, the war on terrorism altered the political environment in Indonesia and in some ways increased the vulnerability of her government. The key factor in her government's survival and possibly in the future of Indonesia as a secular and democratic state may be how well the Indonesian political, religious, and military establishments handle the resurgence of militant Islam.

---

[1]This thought is articulated in Peters (2002). Peters is an author and retired U.S. Army lieutenant colonel.

An open confrontation with radical Islamic militants could destabilize the Indonesian government as it goes into the 2004 presidential election, but a passive stance could be interpreted as a sign of weakness and could be equally destabilizing.

These dynamics create tension in U.S. policy toward Indonesia. Indonesia's full cooperation in the global war on terrorism is important to U.S. interests, but if Jakarta presses too hard on the issue of the war on terrorism, those actions could prove to be counterproductive to maintaining political stability in Indonesia. In the long term, Indonesia's continued stability and the survival of its secular democratic government are of overriding interest.

Whatever course the Jakarta government, the political parties, and other actors in the Indonesian drama take, the military will play a key role in charting that course. As an institution, the military remained neutral in the events that led to the fall of Suharto, the Habibie interregnum, and the election of Abdurrahman Wahid, and supported Megawati's accession to the presidency. The Indonesian National Military (Tentara Nasional Indonesia, or TNI), however, is not ideologically neutral. It views itself as the repository of the values embodied in the nation's secular ideology, *Pancasila,* and as the guardian of its unity and territorial integrity. For all of its faults, the Indonesian military throughout its history has been representative of all of the different ethnic and religious components of the Indonesian nation.

The military has always been distrustful of political Islam—partially as the result of its experience in fighting Islamist revolts in the late 1940s and 1950s and because the military regards political Islam as a threat to its vision of a unified multicultural Indonesia. However, the military is not immune to the trends that influence the larger society. A widening of the ethno-religious divides in Indonesian society will affect military cohesion as well. How the military responds to the challenges of upholding democracy, secularism, and unity and to the stresses of change within its own institution, and how the United States can help Indonesia deal positively with these challenges, constitute the themes of this report.

This report is divided into three parts:

Part I (Chapters Two through Seven) discusses the origins and institutional development of the Indonesian armed forces from the country's independence to the present day. Chapters Two through Four discuss force structure, doctrine, and the intelligence function. Chapter Five deals with the changing political role of the military. This chapter will be of interest to political analysts and students of broader political trends in Indonesia. Chapter Six is a look at the TNI from within; it covers officer recruitment, career patterns, military education and training, promotions, ethnicity, religion, and military cohesion. This chapter seeks to answer the key analytical question of whether there are cracks in the solid front that the military attempts to convey that might destabilize the institution. Chapter Seven discusses the obscure but important area of the military's funding and economic interests.

Part II (Chapters Eight through Ten) analyzes the security challenges confronting Indonesia and the Indonesian government and military's response to these challenges. Chapter Eight looks at the threat of terrorism and religious extremism. Chapter Nine deals with the communal violence in central and eastern Indonesia and the role of "jihadist" organizations in this conflict. Chapter Ten deals with what is perhaps of greatest concern to the authorities in Jakarta—the secessionist movements in Aceh and Papua.

Part III (Chapters Eleven through Thirteen) is devoted to the issue of the U.S.–Indonesian bilateral military relationship. Chapter Eleven provides a history and assessment of, as the chapter's title says, the "rocky course" of U.S.–Indonesian military relations. It describes the congressional restrictions on U.S. military assistance to Indonesia over the past decade and analyzes the effects of the restriction on U.S. influence and access to the Indonesian military and on Indonesian military professionalism. Chapter Twelve outlines various possible future Indonesian scenarios—from democratic consolidation to radical Islamic influence or control, or territorial disintegration—and their implications for U.S. interests and regional security. Chapter Thirteen concludes the report with a series of goals for Indonesian military reform and elements of a U.S. strategy of engagement with Indonesia. The appendix provides an assessment of the progress that Indonesia has made in meeting the requirements of the Leahy amendment, the provision in the U.S. appropriations legislation that blocks some kinds of U.S. military assistance to Indonesia.

PART I: THE TNI

Chapter Two

ORIGINS AND INSTITUTIONAL DEVELOPMENT OF THE INDONESIAN ARMED FORCES

THE FOUNDING OF THE ARMED FORCES

Indonesia came into being as the successor state to the Netherlands East Indies, a sprawling colonial empire of more than 14,000 islands between the Asian mainland and Australia. The Dutch had cobbled together this empire over a period of 300 years from an array of independent indigenous states and sultanates. From the beginning, the army held a unique position in the state because of its instrumental role in securing Indonesia's independence from the Dutch.

The Indonesian national military, TNI, was officially established on October 5, 1945, to defend the Republic's independence, which had been proclaimed on August 17, 1945, two days after the Japanese surrender to the Allies. The origin of the Indonesian army was in the pro-independence militia formations organized by Indonesian nationalists after the Japanese surrender in 1945. The core of the army was organized and directed by the charismatic and legendary General Sudirman, who became commander of the fledging independence fighters while still in his 20s and who died of tuberculosis just one month after independence was achieved in December 1949. Sudirman, revered still to this day, provided the basic doctrine of the army—a guerrilla force that stung the Dutch colonial army but rarely engaged in set-piece battles.

Most of the officers, including Sudirman and a young lieutenant colonel (later president) Suharto, came from the PETA (Pasukan

Sukarela Tentara Pembela Tanah Air, or Defenders of the Fatherland) the territorial army organized by the Japanese during the occupation.[1] Some of those officers had received military training in the KNIL (Koninklijk Nederlandsch–Indische Leger), the Netherlands East Indies Army; others were members of politically oriented militia (*laskar*) formations. Most were Javanese and nonorthodox (or *abangan*) Muslims, but some laskar units were leftist or communist. These political divisions were to bring about a war within the war for independence.

On December 19, 1948, the Dutch attacked the Republican capital of Yogyakarta and captured Sukarno and the Republican civilian leadership. The army, under General Sudirman, refused to surrender and waged an ultimately successful guerrilla war against the Dutch. The army's perseverance in the armed struggle, contrasted with the perceived ineffectiveness of the civilians, gave rise to the perception of the army as the institution that preserved the Indonesian nation and provided the rationale for the military's special role in politics. While carrying on the war against the Dutch, the military was also instrumental in defeating internal threats to the Republic, notably the Madiun rebellion, launched by the Indonesian Communist Party on September 18, 1948.

The agreements accompanying the Dutch recognition of Indonesia's independence in December 1949 provided for a federal system (the "United States of Indonesia"). Indonesia's founding president Sukarno and other nationalists, however, worked to replace the federal system with a unitary system and to concentrate power in the central government in Jakarta. In 1950, the federal system was abol-

---

[1]The Java PETA was organized with a strength of 70 battalions in Java, Madura, and Bali and 55 companies in Sumatra. The units in Java, Madura, and Bali were under the command of the 16th Japanese army, while the *Giyugun* in Sumatra was under the 25th army. These and all other pro-Japanese indigenous military units in Southeast Asia were designated by the Japanese as *Kyodo Bo-ei Giyugun,* or "voluntary army to protect the native land." Japanese strategists anticipated using indigenous forces to resist Allied landings. In the last year of occupation, the Japanese set up intensive guerrilla warfare courses for PETA officers, who in turn trained 900 troops in Java alone in guerrilla tactics, counterintelligence, and territorial control. After the Japanese surrender, the Japanese authorities, on instructions from the Allies, ordered the disbandment of PETA. These instructions were ignored by the Indonesian nationalists, who proclaimed the independence of the Republic on August 17, 1945 ("The Genesis of the Indonesian National Army ...," n.d.).

ished, after the central government's forces overcame local resistance in South Sulawesi and the Moluccas. Continued disaffection with Jakarta's centralism in some of the outlying provinces provoked the outbreak of regionalist rebellions in eastern Indonesia in 1957 and western Sumatra in 1958, in which locally based military units participated.

The role of Islam in the state was the other key issue confronting Indonesia's founders. After independence, disagreements between those who advocated an Islamic state and those who wanted to establish the new Republic on a secular basis[2] were resolved in favor of the latter. The 1945 constitution included Pancasila, which defined the national identity without reference to Islam, as the national ideology.[3] Pancasila and the 1945 constitution were and remain the "sole basis" of the politics of the Indonesian armed forces (McFarling, 2001).[4] In response, radical Muslims who refused to recognize the authority of the Indonesian state launched the Darul Islam rebellion on West Java in 1948. The rebellion spread to Aceh and South Sulawesi in the 1950s and continued until the 1960s.

MILITARY CULTURE AND DOCTRINE

The basic TNI doctrine places primary emphasis on the army, the dominant service in the Indonesian military. Both the air force and the navy are charged with providing direct support to the army, with their individual service missions secondary in importance. The army prides itself on its history as a revolutionary people's army and as the prime mover of Indonesia's independence. Consequently, the military came to view itself as the guardian of national unity and cohe-

---

[2]"Secular," in the Indonesian context, is defined as being based on Pancasila (see Footnote 3).

[3]The word Pancasila translates to "five principles." Those principles are (1) belief in "the One and Only God," (2) a just and civilized humanity, (3) the unity of Indonesia, (4) democracy, and (5) social justice (from the Preamble to the 1945 Indonesian Constitution [Undang-Undang Dasar 1945]).

[4](Briefing by Group Captain Ian McFarling, Royal Australian Air Force, Arlington, Va. April 20, 2001.) The *Sapta Marga* (Seven Pledges), the code of conduct of the armed forces that was formulated in 1951, says that "the Army (armed forces) in no way discerns or adheres to any political creed (belief/system/doctrine)." However, Sapta Marga requires the military to defend Pancasila.

sion and as a co-equal to the civilian political leadership (some Indonesian military advocates note that the establishment of the army predated that of the Republic). In contrast to armies in other Southeast Asian states—such as the Thai and Philippine armies—the Indonesian army developed an ideological and legal framework to support a formal role in political affairs, originally called "middle road" and later renamed *dwifungsi,* or dual function. This concept held that the military had a "sociopolitical" as well as a defense function and gave the military an institutionalized role in politics.

The concept of the "middle road" was formally enunciated by the army chief of staff General Abdul Haris Nasution in a speech to the army's Officers Training College in 1958 and developed in seminars at the Indonesian General Staff and Command College in the 1960s.[5] Nasution argued that the armed forces were neither "a tool of civilian society" as in Western countries, nor a "military regime" that dominates the state, but a force of the people, working with other forces of the people. After Suharto and the military assumed power in 1966, dwifungsi became official policy. Beginning in 1966, the government enacted a series of laws to define the role of the military in governmental and national affairs (Sidwell, 1995). The military was given corporate representation in the parliament and active and retired military officers served in positions in the cabinet, the civil administration, and state corporations. The paradigm not only permitted, but also demanded, that officers take an active part in politics to ensure stability and central control.

The dual function dovetailed with the doctrine of "total people's defense" (*Sishankamrata*), a Maoist-style concept of people's war that contemplated mass mobilization to defend the country against external or internal threat. The doctrine assumes that a nation as diverse and as dependent on vulnerable air and sea lines of communication as Indonesia is could not be centrally defended. Total people's defense was meant to ensure that even if the center were overrun (as in the case of the Dutch capture of the Republican leadership in 1948) resistance would continue. The doctrine calls on the army to fight an invading force as a guerrilla army, wearing the enemy down

---

[5]General Nasution later became disillusioned by the way in which Suharto changed and implemented dwifungsi and became an influential critic of the system in his later years.

through guerrilla tactics until stronger allies arrive to assist or the invader finds the effort too difficult to sustain.

The basic national defense strategy recognizes that there is very little threat of a conventional attack by outside forces. Indeed, no country besides the United States has the capability to mount a conventional amphibious invasion. For an outside power to prevail, it must have the support of a major part of the population. Even during the Indonesian Revolution, the KNIL was a predominantly indigenous soldiery with mainly Dutch and a few local officers. In the most serious challenges to national survival—the regionalist Permesta revolt in East Indonesia and the contemporaneous rebellion in Sumatra by the anti-Sukarnoist Revolutionary Government of the Republic of Indonesia (PRRI) from 1957 to 1959, and the abortive coup d'état of October 1965—the main danger was from disaffected army units supported by a significant segment of the population. From this history, the military leadership has drawn the conclusion that internal cohesion in the army and the support of the population are the main elements of national survival.

The operational concept for a successful conventional defense of the nation is for the outer islands to absorb the initial blow, and local resources to be mobilized and reinforced by the air and naval power available. The Army Strategic Reserve Command (Kostrad) will reinforce the forward defense, mobilize and train additional forces, and prepare the heartland—Java—for the main battle.[6]

The emphasis on guerrilla tactics calls for the military to maintain intimately detailed knowledge of Indonesia's terrain, people, resources, and infrastructure. Given the diversity of these factors across Indonesia's great breadth, the TNI doctrine calls for an ubiquitous military presence everywhere to collect and store the necessary intelligence for guerrilla warfare and, most important, to establish the rapport with the local population that would enable the TNI to operate in accordance with classic Maoist and Yugoslav doc-

---

[6]The authors are grateful to Colonel Charles D. McFetridge (U.S. Army, retired) for his helpful assistance in outlining the TNI and army strategic and tactical doctrine. A graduate of the Indonesian Army Command and Staff School (Sesko AD), Colonel McFetridge served as U.S. Defense and Army Attaché to Indonesia from 1994 to 1998. His contributions are reflected throughout this chapter.

trine.[7] The reality, of course, particularly in the restive provinces of Aceh and Irian Jaya, was different.

The TNI doctrine is supported by a territorial command structure of 12 military area commands (Komando Daerah Militer or Kodam), each theoretically responsible for the independent defense of a part of the archipelago (see Figure 2.1 for the locations of the Kodam).[8] Like dwifungsi, the concepts behind the territorial system were developed in seminars in the 1950s and early 1960s. While at the General Staff and Command College in 1960, Suharto was one of the participants at a seminar in which the establishment of a parallel structure to the civil administration was first discussed.[9] The structure was developed primarily to counter an internal threat from a communist insurgency. Under Suharto's "New Order" regime, the territorial command system was used to maintain Suharto in power and monitor the activities of religious organizations, student organizations, trade unions, and other nongovernmental organizations that could become sources of dissident activity.

MILITARY ORGANIZATION AND DEPLOYMENT

The army historically has been the dominant service in the Indonesian military.[10] Former president Abdurrahman Wahid prioritized a major expansion of the navy and the marine corps to protect mari-

---

[7]In correspondence with Angel Rabasa, TNI historian Ken Conboy noted the important influence that the Yugoslav model exercised over the Indonesian concept of a "people's war." Conboy cited A. H. Nasution's comments about the Yugoslav resistance during the Second World War. Nasution mentioned that Tito was widely known in Indonesia since the time of the Indonesian revolution, spoke in positive terms about the Yugoslav system of self-reliance, and stated that the Indonesian concept of total people's defense mirrors the Yugoslav system. (See Nasution, 1985.) Conboy also notes that many Indonesian officers, including half a dozen who became prominent generals, attended war college and staff college in Yugoslavia prior to 1965.

[8]The territorial system includes the newly reestablished unnumbered Kodam in the Moluccas (2001) and Kodam Iskandar Muda in Aceh (2002). Both had been disestablished in a major consolidation and reorganization of the military command structure in 1986.

[9]These concepts became the Territorial Management and Civic Mission doctrines (McDonald, 1980, p. 34).

[10]This section of the chapter is partially based on the personal experiences of Colonel John Haseman (U.S. Army, retired) and Colonel Charles D. McFetridge in their tours as U.S. Defense Attachés in Indonesia and on other sources as cited.

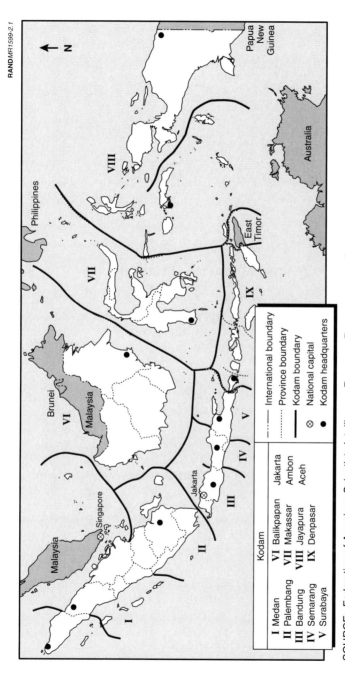

RAND*MR1599-2.1*

Kodam

I Medan	VI Balikpapan	Jakarta
II Palembang	VII Makassar	Ambon
III Bandung	VIII Jayapura	Aceh
IV Semarang	IX Denpasar	
V Surabaya		

----- International boundary
········· Province boundary
——— Kodam boundary
⊗ National capital
● Kodam headquarters

SOURCE: Federation of American Scientists Intelligence Resource Program at www.fas.org.

NOTES: Jakarta has its own Kodam known as Jaya. There are also two unnumbered Kodam, the Iskandar Muda command at Aceh and the Security Restoration Operations Command at Ambon. Boundary representation is not necessarily authoritative.

Figure 2.1—Military Command Areas (Kodam)

time resources and improve the military's strategic mobility capability. However, implementing these priorities has been impossible because of a lack of resources.

Apart from the important political issues involved, given the doctrinal background of the Indonesian army, its structure and deployment are based on sound considerations. The Indonesian army characterizes its forces as "tactical" and "territorial." Approximately one-quarter of the army's strength is assigned to its two major tactical commands, Kostrad (approximately 27,000 personnel) and the Special Forces Command (Kopassus) (about 5,000 personnel). About two-thirds of the army's strength is assigned to the territorial system; the remainder is in army headquarters' staff, schools, and technical units and centers.

Army Strategic Reserve Command (Kostrad)

Kostrad's fighting strength lies in 33 combat battalions organized into two divisions with five infantry brigades and one separate airborne brigade which comes directly under Kostrad headquarters (see Figure 2.2). The two divisions are headquartered on Java, and the separate brigade is in South Sulawesi. Each division has both airborne and infantry brigades. Kostrad rotates alert status among its brigades and designates one battalion in rotating order for immediate deployment to meet security contingencies anywhere in the country. Kostrad battalions are available on a standard basis for service in troubled areas on longer deployments, usually 12 months or longer in duration.[11] All of Kostrad's battalions have been repetitively deployed in recent years to the primary security challenges in East Timor, Aceh, the Moluccas, and Papua.

TNI doctrine calls for Kostrad to be the nation's second line of defense and primary reinforcement against any outside threat. A similar approach is used to deal with internal instability. The local military command relies on available resources to contain and defuse the threat with territorial battalions used in civic action programs, while the Kodam ready-reaction battalion or battalions confront the

---

[11]At present, deployments to Papua and Aceh are 12-month tours.

RAND*MR1599-2.2*

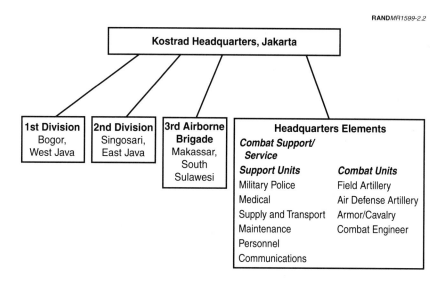

Figure 2.2—Kostrad Organization

armed enemy. If the Kodam cannot handle the problem with forces on hand, Kostrad units, assisted by air and naval elements as appropriate, reinforce the Kodam. Thus, Kostrad has been used almost exclusively as the national reaction force against guerrilla threats in East Timor and Aceh, to put down riots and other civil disturbances, and most recently to respond to sectarian and religious violence in such places as the Moluccas and Central Sulawesi. The key to success in either case, according to TNI doctrine, is support of the population, without which neither a prolonged conventional defense nor a successful counterinsurgency can be accomplished.

Consequently, improving discipline and understanding of the rules of engagement among troops deployed to conflict area has been a key priority of senior army officers. According to former army deputy chief of staff Lieutenant General Kiki Syahnakri, 60 percent of the training is focused on understanding the rules of engagement and avoiding civilian casualties. The TNI has also issued written guidelines for troops sent to the field. The guidelines provide basic instruction in combat situations, with emphasis on rules of engagement and respect for human rights ("Military Professionalism Pays Off …," 2002).

Since the early 1990s, the TNI has made ambitious plans to expand Kostrad to three full divisions, most likely building upon the separate brigade on Sulawesi (Lowry, 1996, p. 22). However, the government has never made funds available for such a major expansion and the plan remains unfulfilled. As is, Kostrad has priority for weapons and equipment over the territorial battalions and cultivates unit loyalty by allowing qualified personnel to remain in Kostrad assignments throughout most of their careers.

The army chief of staff is responsible for the recruitment, training, and equipping of Kostrad and its personnel. However, Kostrad is directly under the armed forces commander's operational control. Thus, it is the TNI, and not the army, that gives Kostrad its mission, deployment orders, and operational guidance. In this regard, operational control of Kostrad is very much like the chain of command over U.S. Army divisions, without the intervening level of the unified command.

Army Special Forces Command (Kopassus)

The Indonesian army's most elite unit is Kopassus. Its 5,000 personnel are very well trained, superbly conditioned, have strong esprit de corps, and are linked by personal ties to charismatic commanders. Kopassus personnel are trained and organized for both traditional special forces missions—infiltration, guerrilla and counterguerrilla warfare, training, and counterterrorism—and covert and intelligence operations throughout the country. Kopassus units are permanently garrisoned on Java, but operational teams are maintained continuously in the same troubled regions where Kostrad units are deployed.

Kopassus historically has been the most frequently deployed component of the force structure. Those deployments have generally involved small task force (seldom larger than two companies), team, and individual deployments on intelligence gathering; reinforcement to larger tactical units; and "black" (covert) operations. Kopassus deployments range in length from a few days to many months. Long-term missions, such as those in East Timor, were usually accomplished by rotating different units with short overlaps for operational familiarization and handoff to the replacement unit. Kopassus has never, to the knowledge of any observers, deployed its operational groups in toto.

Kopassus personnel are tough, ruthless soldiers who have been accused or suspected of numerous human rights violations over the past 15 years. In many cases, it is not known whether these abuses were perpetrated by rogue elements acting out of personal loyalty to officers involved in unauthorized activities or by personnel responding to orders given through the chain of command. In any case, up to the present time, Kopassus personnel have effectively been protected from investigation and prosecution for wrongdoing. A notable exception was the 1999 Honor Court and forced retirement of Lieutenant General Prabowo Subianto, a long-time special forces officer and later Kopassus and then Kostrad commander, and the subsequent courts-martial of several of his former subordinates for a series of political abductions in 1998. General Prabowo's estrangement from many senior TNI officers also contributed to his downfall.

Kopassus has undergone several reorganizations during the past 15 years. The most recent, in 2001, confirmed its current strength at approximately 5,000 soldiers in an organization including three operational groups (see Figure 2.3). Kopassus organization reflects traditional special operations structures seen elsewhere, with the key element being a small operational team. These teams usually consist of 10 to 15 personnel but are routinely formed into whatever size team is needed to accomplish the assigned mission. Command of Kopassus teams, companies, battalions, or groups is an avidly sought posting. Successful commanders are usually assured of rapid career advancement to the general officer rank.

RAND*MR1599-2.3*

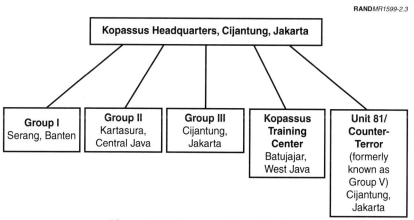

Figure 2.3—Kopassus Organization

Territorial Forces

The bulk of the army's personnel is assigned to the territorial forces. Personnel are assigned to either the territorial structure or the dozens of combat arms and combat support battalions assigned to the territorial organization. Around 150,000 troops are assigned to these forces (International Crisis Group [ICG], 2000b, p. 22).

By doctrine, each Kodam has at least one infantry battalion under direct Kodam control. At least one battalion per Kodam is assigned the Kodam quick-reaction mission, maintaining an alert readiness posture to respond to natural calamities or civil unrest in the Kodam area of responsibility. These units may be airborne infantry battalions, although in recent years the percentage of combat troops who are in fact airborne-qualified has declined.[12] In some cases, the best available security may be provided by cavalry, field artillery, or air defense artillery units.

The Kodam quick-reaction battalions are usually well trained because of the nature of their mission. The professional level of the other territorial battalions varies widely, and is dependent on the resources available to the applicable command, the amount of attention given to the units by the chain of command, and on other training, resource, and personnel constraints. Even these units, however, are called upon to deploy to troubled regions for operational commitments. For example, every territorial infantry battalion, except those from Papua, were eventually sent to East Timor for a yearlong deployment during the military campaign there.

The kodam are divided into Komando Resor Militer (Military Resor[13] Commands or Korem), with at least one infantry battalion each. Korem, in turn, are divided into Komando Distrik Militer (Military District Commands or Kodim) headed by a lieutenant colonel, and districts are divided into Komando Rayon Militer (Military Subdistrict Commands or Koramil) with a junior officer or non-commissioned officer (NCO) in charge. In theory, every village has a noncommissioned officer (*Babinsa*) assigned. In practice, an NCO

---

[12]Since 1999, all but three Kodam battalions have lost their airborne designation and have reverted to infantry battalions.

[13]There is no satisfactory English translation of the Indonesian military term "Resor."

can be responsible for several villages. Large Korem and those in which important industrial centers are located have several assigned battalions. The air defense artillery battalions, for example, are assigned to defend such areas as the Lhokseumawe industrial zone in Aceh and the Bontang and Balikpapan industrial areas in East Kalimantan (see Table 2.1 for the numbers of various types of tactical units in the command structure).

The missions of the territorial battalions span a number of traditional and less conventional duties. They are assigned the static security mission for strategic centers. In the area around Lhokseumawe, Aceh, several battalions have reinforced organic units that are assigned to static defense of the huge ExxonMobil natural gas fields and the state oil company Pertamina refinery against the threat posed by the separatist Gerakan Aceh Merdeka (GAM), or Free Aceh Movement. ExxonMobil halted its operations and evacuated its staff for several months in 2001 because of the threat to its employees, costing Indonesia $100 million per month in lost revenue.

Some territorial battalions maintain high standards of training and soldierly proficiency and are capable of meeting any tactical requirements that may be assigned to them. Many units, however, are not at a high level of readiness, and virtually all territorial units operate below their authorized strength. A primary reason for these shortcomings, of course, is that priority in meeting personnel requirements is given to Kostrad and Kopassus. In addition to the shortage of resources, the corruption, the diversion of assets, and other problems that plague the territorial forces, territorial units suffer from depleted personnel strength because of the large number of

Table 2.1

Tactical Units in the Territorial Structure

Kodam	Korem	Kodim	Infantry Battalions	Cavalry Battalions	Field Artillery Battalions	Air Defense Artillery Battalions
12	39	271	66	8	8	8

SOURCE: Lowry, 1996.

NOTE: Tactical deployment requirements frequently change the number of battalions available within any one particular Kodam area of responsibility.

soldiers who are assigned additional employment in the civilian sector in order to supplement their salaries (see Chapter Six for a further discussion).

The territorial battalions have borne the brunt of internal stability missions in the past and continue to play an important role in maintaining public order despite the transfer of that responsibility to the national police in 1999. The reaction capabilities of these units vary enormously depending on their quality of leadership, logistical support, equipment, and training. Few territorial battalions have crowd-control equipment and training. For a young commander with such constraints, the choices available in the event of major civil disturbances are bleak: Shoot rioters or allow the violence to run its course.

Naval and Air Forces

The army has always been the politically dominant service in Indonesia. Until the appointment of Admiral Widodo Adisutjipto as armed forces chief during the Wahid administration, all armed forces commanders in chief had been army officers and the army very much set military policy. Nevertheless, as an archipelagic country with more than 14,000 islands and a coastline of 55,000 kilometers, Indonesia is dependent on the navy and the air force to maintain inter-island communications and transport troops and military stores. The 1957 to 1959 rebellions in Sumatra and Sulawesi were put down with the help of air power, and today, air transport is a critical element in the central government's ability to respond quickly to outbreaks of communal conflict in the outer islands.[14]

There are two operational naval commands, the Eastern Fleet, based in Surabaya, and the Western Fleet, with headquarters in Jakarta. Indonesia's naval forces consist of 17 main frigate-size combatants, 36 patrol and coastal combatants, including 16 unseaworthy former East German corvettes, missile and torpedo craft, 26 landing craft, 12 mine countermeasures craft that are mainly used for coastal patrol,

---

[14]TNI historian Ken Conboy points out that while air power played a role in the suppression of the rebellions, ground forces were the decisive factor, and the vast majority of the troops were moved by sea (correspondence with Ken Conboy, June 2002).

and two German T-209/1300 submarines. Vessels in operational condition are deployed in what are considered to be key sea-lanes or sensitive areas, such as the Strait of Malacca, the waters around Aceh, and the Makassar Strait. The navy has also been tasked with sealing off violence-torn islands in the Moluccas. It also has some naval air capabilities, including antisubmarine warfare and search-and-rescue helicopters. There is a Military Sealift Command, with some amphibious and transport ships used for inter-island communication and logistical support of the army and navy, and a marine corps, about 12,000 strong, with two combat infantry regiments, one stationed with each of the fleets.

The air force has two operational commands or Ko-Ops. Ko-Op I, headquartered in Jakarta, is responsible for operations west of Jakarta; and Ko-Op II, at Makassar (formerly Ujung Pandang) in South Sulawesi, is responsible for operations east of Jakarta. The air force has a territorial defense mission, conducts strategic surveillance of the waters around Indonesia, transports ground forces and equipment, and carries out humanitarian relief missions. The air force's combat strength consists of one squadron of F-16A/Bs, based at Madiun-Iswahyudi air base, in Java, and two squadrons of BAe Hawk Mk 109/209 and one squadron of Hawk Mk 53 light attack aircraft based at Supadio air base, in Pontianak, West Kalimantan, and at Simpang Tiga, in Sumatra. There is also one squadron of refurbished A-4Es based at Hasanuddin, near Makassar, a squadron of aging Israeli-supplied A-4Es based in Pekan Baru, in central Sumatra, and Makassar, and one squadron of upgraded F-5E/Fs near the end of their useful life at Madiun-Iswahyudi. In addition, there is also one reconnaissance squadron of 12 OV-10F aircraft and one wing (three aircraft) of B-737s used for sea surveillance. The air force also operates two squadrons of C-130s and a number of smaller transport and rotary-wing aircraft.[15]

The 1997–1998 Asian economic crisis hit Indonesia particularly hard and devastated ambitious military modernization and readiness plans. The air force and the navy, which are more dependent on ac-

---

[15]Sources for the description of the Indonesian naval and air forces are "Cutting Closer to the Bone," 2001; *Jane's World Air Forces,* 2001, pp. 182–183; and International Institute for Strategic Studies 2002, pp. 191–193. Data on Indonesia's navy and air force are from Periscope data service, www.periscope.ucg.com.

cess to technology and spare parts than is the army, were dispropor-
tionately affected. In June 1997, the Suharto government cancelled
plans to purchase seven F-16As and two F-16Bs—originally built for
Pakistan—because of U.S. congressional criticism of Indonesia's
record on human rights and East Timor. Subsequent plans to acquire
12 Russian SU-30MK and eight Mi-17 helicopters were suspended
after the onset of the economic crisis. Budgetary constraints forced
President Wahid's defense minister Juwono Sudarsono to impose a
moratorium on the purchase of major capital equipment. Whatever
funding was available beyond personnel expenses was to go for
maintenance of existing equipment.[16] Nevertheless, the deterioration of air force and naval capabilities has deepened. According to
Indonesian air force officials, the budget covers only 8 percent of
maintenance requirements. As of April 2002, only 3 of the original 12
F-16 aircraft and 7 of 19 C-130 transport aircraft are operational and
the air force has reduced flying hours to below minimum requirements.[17]

MILITARY OPERATIONS

According to Indonesian army doctrine, there are three kinds of operations: combat operations, intelligence operations, and territorial
operations. To seize an area controlled by an enemy, the military
conducts intelligence or combat operations. Intelligence operations
are covert in nature and conducted by intelligence units. Territorial
operations are carried out by combat or territorial units and have the
purpose of restoring political, economic, or social order. The TNI
doctrine differentiated between two kinds of territorial operations:
"construction" operations and "opposition/resistance" operations.
Construction operations involve civic action. They are designed to
improve conditions in areas considered to be at risk of political and
social instability. The military is employed in civic action projects
such as construction of housing, schools, dams, irrigation systems,
and in the introduction of modern farming systems. In some of the
outer islands, these projects were implemented in connection with

---

[16]Interview with former Defense Minister Juwono Sudarsono, Jakarta, February 8,
2002.

[17]Discussions with Indonesian military officers, Jakarta, February 2002.

the transmigration program, which involved the resettlement of people from heavily populated areas, generally in Java and Madura, to other parts of the archipelago. Construction operations were performed routinely by territorial units or sometimes as part of targeted efforts to reduce the appeal of insurgent groups.

If construction and intelligence operations fail to prevent the development of a threat such as an insurgency, the Indonesian military will conduct opposition/resistance operations. In the first phase, the military forces concentrate their combat power to eliminate the physical presence of the enemy in what is called the *annihilation zone*. As the military gains limited control of this area, it is designated as a *consolidation zone*. When opposition influence wanes, the area is redesignated as a *stabilization zone*. Here "construction" operations are undertaken to reconstruct damaged infrastructure and regain the confidence of the population. When the area is completely pacified, it is redesignated as a *rear area*. After government control is restored, there is a self-correction phase in which the conditions that led the people to revolt are identified and corrected (Sidwell, 1995).

Chapter Three

DOCTRINAL CHANGE: FROM "TOTAL PEOPLE'S DEFENSE AND SECURITY" TO THE "NEW PARADIGM"

There already has been far-reaching change in the decades-long doctrine and organizational structure that are familiar to the entire Indonesian army and TNI hierarchy. At the same time, the looming requirement to adapt, change, and even eliminate missions, organizational structures, and doctrines gleaned throughout the course of a military career has created a stressful environment for military personnel at every level.

There has been a plethora of suggestions from nonmilitary observers as to the changes needed in the structure and organization of the Indonesian military. Some of the most far-reaching changes called for since the fall of Suharto include eliminating the entire territorial structure (because it enshrines the army's political power) and wholesale transfer of army personnel to the marine corps or the police. Neither of these suggestions is practical or feasible, and like many proposals for change in the new evolving democratic Indonesia, they have been made in haste and for the most part without a fully developed analytical basis.

The TNI itself has adopted a new doctrine, which it calls the "New Paradigm." The New Paradigm was developed by a team of senior officers headed by Lieutenant General Susilo Bambang Yudhoyono and was first announced by the armed forces commander, General Wiranto, in August 1998. Harold Crouch, a well-known scholar of the Indonesian military, believes that the new doctrine was the outcome of several years of private discussions by intellectually inclined officers who believed that the armed forces needed to adjust to changes in Indonesian society.[1]

The New Paradigm's goal is to shift the TNI's traditional focus from internal security to external defense. The national police (formerly under the armed forces command) have now been established as a separate organization, reporting directly to the president. The intention of the military reformers was to transfer internal security functions to the national police. According to the new doctrine, the police are to develop paramilitary capabilities to deal with insurgencies and large-scale internal security threats. The TNI is to come to the assistance of the police, at the direction of the central authorities, only if the police cannot handle a situation.

The TNI has been criticized for failing to implement doctrinal and organizational changes more rapidly and effectively. However, there are reasons for the TNI to proceed slowly. The issues at hand require professional and skillful planning from both the civilian and military sectors, but there is a paucity of forward-thinking, reform-minded, capable strategic planners in either sector. The TNI leadership has made several points clear. There will be no change merely for the sake of change. Changes will be implemented only as the larger social and governmental structures are able to absorb them. National unity, public order, and efficient use of scarce resources will be the principal guidelines for military reform (International Crisis Group, 2000b, pp. 13–15).[2]

At the strategic doctrinal level, the major change has already been implemented. The old "Total People's Defense and Security" doctrine (which evolved from the war of independence against the Dutch and lasted until 1998), with its emphasis on guerrilla warfare involving support and assistance from the population and merged ranks of civilian and military cadres, has been formally replaced with the New Paradigm. The separation of the national police from the

---

[1]Conversation with Lieutenant General Susilo Bambang Yudhoyono, Jakarta, February 2002; Crouch, 1999, pp. 137–138.

[2]This point was also made to the authors by high-level military officers and by former Defense Minister Juwono Sudarsono. Juwono noted in an interview that substantive civilian control of the military would depend on the development of viable civilian political structures. (See Chapter Five for a further discussion.)

armed forces was to have ended the army's primary responsibility for internal security and maintenance of public order. Unfortunately, as noted elsewhere in this report, the national police force is insufficiently trained, equipped, or manned to assume the internal security mission. Although, doctrinally, the army is now only a backup force to the police, only the army has the capability to ensure public order and confront armed separatist movements. Indonesia's parliament recognized this by passing legislation in 2001 that assigned four internal security missions to the TNI—operations against separatists, insurgent forces, drug trafficking, and smuggling.

In the view of many experts, the national police will require years of training in paramilitary operations before they can effectively confront insurgents and separatists. The police lack training and equipment, especially nonlethal equipment, for effective crowd and riot control. The army's capabilities will therefore be needed for the foreseeable future. In the past two years, however, the army has demonstrated a curious reluctance to become involved in internal security operations, and has allowed sectarian and religious violence to rage almost uncontrolled for weeks, and in some cases for months.[3]

Many military leaders believe that the inability of the police to assume the domestic security mission argues for the retention of most, if not all, of the territorial system. They complain that contradictory demands are being placed on the military. It is expected to maintain order, they say, but the central government's directives delegating internal security functions to the national police have their hands tied. They argue that the projection of military power through the territorial system would reduce the level of violence seen during the past several years. As could be expected, many observers and critics point to exactly the same thinking as the reason why the military has reacted slowly and ineffectively to outbreaks of communal violence.

---

[3]Since the fall of Suharto, there has been a noticeable decline in the military's willingness to take aggressive action to quell civil violence. With the military under greater scrutiny with regard to human rights practices, local commanders may have become more risk-adverse and less willing to use force against violent civilian elements, particularly if these elements represent politically influential forces. It should be mentioned that TNI doctrine calls for the territorial commander to develop a wide network of contacts with community leaders. By using force against civilians the commander risks alienating the very people on whose cooperation the success of his mission may depend. (See Chapter Nine for more information.)

Obviously, this conflict between reality and doctrinal change must be resolved at the national political level, but until that happens, the specter of continued violence is a real threat in virtually every region of Indonesia.

A great deal of the debate on military reform in the heyday of *reformasi*[4] centered on the future of the army's territorial structure. Speaking to military commanders and retired generals in March 2000, Army Chief of Staff Tyasno Sudarto conceded that past mistakes had sparked calls for the TNI to reform its territorial mission. Sudarto said that the TNI would revamp its structure and reduce the number of military commands to a minimum ("TNI to Study …," 2000). The TNI conducted several workshops in 2001 to examine options for adjusting or withdrawing from the territorial structure (International Crisis Group, 2001d, p. 5). At a meeting of senior military officers in October 2001, there was agreement that the army would gradually withdraw from its territorial function, but that conditions in some areas were not yet conducive to the end of the military's territorial role. The army's view was that it would be a matter of years before a transfer of territorial functions to the civilian authorities could be accomplished ("Territorial Shift …," 2001).[5]

As part of this process, the TNI announced the downgrading of the position of chief of staff for territorial affairs to an assistant post under the chief of staff for general affairs. The former territorial affairs chief, Lieutenant General Agus Widjojo, suggested that the transfer of functions should be conducted gradually, starting from the lowest levels of the territorial structure at the regency (district) and lower levels ("TNI to Downgrade …," 2001). First to close would be units where an adequate civilian infrastructure is in place—for instance, in large cities such as Jakarta and Surabaya. More rural and isolated units will remain in operation until such an infrastructure is

---

[4]*Reformasi* is the term used in Indonesia to characterize the political reforms that followed the fall of Suharto's New Order.

[5]During a conversation in Jakarta in June 2002 with a senior TNI officer, the officer pointed out that the territorial structure is actually the military's basing structure, and that it provides flexibility, compensates for lack of mobility, and is essential to monitoring the subversive groups that are now the main threat to Indonesia's national security.

developed, which means some units will remain operational for the foreseeable future.

Suggestions have been made that much of the manpower for an expanded Kostrad, marine corps, and national police can be found by downsizing or demobilizing the army's territorial structure and transferring the resulting surplus personnel. However, in addition to the training costs of producing qualified officers and soldiers for Kostrad, the marine corps, or the national police, most of the resulting personnel would consist of experienced but older NCOs and older junior-ranking officers graduated from the Officer Candidate School *(Secapa)*. These officers usually are not commissioned as second lieutenants until they are in their late 20s or early 30s and are not considered suitable for assignment to the tactical units. Similarly, the age of the "surplus" personnel would make them unsuitable for service in the marine corps. Few of them want to be reassigned to the police, which might actually be a more practical and effective use of their politically oriented skills and local knowledge.

For these reasons, wholesale transfers from territorial units to boost the strength of the tactical units are not feasible. Once a reduction in force is implemented by eliminating Babinsa, Koramil, or Kodim staff positions, many of those affected could be offered early retirement or may voluntarily resign to retain the secondary employment positions most of them already hold. Those who do not choose resignation or retirement could be reassigned to other territorial units in the same geographic area. Thus, sergeants from village posts and the officers and NCOs at the Koramil level could be taken into the applicable Korem and Kodam battalions. This would result in a higher percentage of manpower in the territorial battalions, but would not necessarily produce any major improvement in the readiness of those units.

Fully implementing the new doctrine will require enormous changes in the TNI's culture, organizational structure, training, and personnel practices. From a practical standpoint, the military transformation envisioned by the new doctrine would also require resources to reequip and retrain the Indonesian armed forces that are not currently available. However, the key factor in the future of Indonesian military reform is whether the cultural change that is needed to move the reform process forward has taken place. Lieutenant General

Widjojo observed that there is a great of confusion and disorientation within the TNI because the spirit of the reforms has not been communicated clearly within the chain of command, and because the reforms have not been supported by competent civilian leadership. The reform program, in Widjojo's view, was developed at the higher headquarters, but did not filter down. Moreover, he said, there are continued links between retired senior officers and active-duty army officers. The influence of these officers, and their agendas, acts as a brake on reforms.[6]

The future of military reform in Indonesia is therefore highly uncertain. At the present time, the majority view in the TNI remains in favor of gradual change within a democratic political framework. However, the momentum for reform appears to be diminishing under the weight of institutional inertia and the practical difficulties in implementing strategic change. Nevertheless, as Widjojo also pointed out, the military reformers have succeeded in projecting the issue of military reform outside of military channels, to nongovernmental organizations (NGOs), think tanks, the parliament, and other government agencies.[7] Therefore, in a democratic Indonesia, where military matters will no longer be the exclusive preserve of the TNI, pressures from civil society could reinforce the impetus for change within the military.

---

[6]Interview with Lieutenant General Agus Widjojo, Jakarta, June 2002. At the time of the interview, Widjojo was Deputy Speaker of the Majelis Permusyawaratan Rakyat (MPR, the People's Consultative Assembly).

[7]Interview with Lieutenant General Agus Widjojo, Jakarta, June 2002.

Chapter Four

CHANGES IN THE INTELLIGENCE FUNCTION

Besides the armed forces and the police, the intelligence agencies constitute the third pillar of Indonesia's security apparatus. Under Suharto, the intelligence function resided in a plethora of organizations, the most important of which were the Strategic Intelligence Agency, Badan Intelijen Strategis (BAIS), responsible for military and foreign intelligence (through its control of the Indonesian defense attachés), and the State Intelligence Coordinating Board, Badan Koordinasi Intelijen Negara (BAKIN), redesignated the state intelligence agency, Badan Intelijen Negara (BIN), after the fall of Suharto. In addition, each army Kodam has an intelligence staff that reports through the Assistant for Intelligence to the Army Chief of Staff and then the Armed Forces Commander.

In the latter Suharto years, BAIS and BAKIN personnel also staffed the Agency for the Coordination of Support for National Stability Development (Bakorstanas), headed by the armed forces commander, which kept track of any political threats to the regime. After Suharto's downfall, Bakorstanas was disbanded (although the staff remained in their home agencies) and the lines of authority in the intelligence community, which in Suharto's New Order regime converged in the person of the president, were thrown into disarray. As of this day, Indonesia lacks a coordinating mechanism for its intelligence agencies. While BAIS reports to TNI headquarters, BIN reports directly to the president. The police, after separation from the armed forces, also report directly to the president.

In this structure, BAIS intelligence could be passed to the president by the armed forces commander at his discretion and BIN intelligence could be passed to the Department (Ministry) of Defense by the president, at least in theory.[1] The Indonesian intelligence structure, therefore, looks roughly like Figure 4.1 (the solid lines indicate chain of command; the dotted line indicates coordination).

BAIS, the military intelligence agency, had been a pervasive part of the power structure under Suharto. It vetted the political loyalty of all government officials and exercised extensive vertical authority through the TNI, routinely bypassing the operational and administrative chain of command. BAIS reached the apogee of its influence in the late 1980s under the directorship of the powerful military leader Leonardus "Benny" Moerdani.[2] For a period after Moerdani's downfall, the armed forces commander (*Panglima*) was dual-hatted as BAIS director. In the backlash against Suharto-era institutions that followed the end of the New Order, the agency was placed under the TNI chief of staff for general affairs, and a nonarmy officer, Air Force Vice Marshal Ian Santoso Perdanakusumah, was appointed as its director (Haseman, 2000).

In its current organization, BAIS is organized into seven directorates, including (1) Internal (Directorate A); (2) Foreign (Directorate B); (3) Defense (Directorate C); (4) Security (Directorate D); (5) Psychological Operations (Directorate E); (6) Budgeting and Administration (Directorate F); and (7) Intelligence Production (Directorate G). The last directorate prepares the intelligence products for the armed forces commander.

BAIS does not have an operational role. Its functions are collection and analysis. BAIS's sources of domestic intelligence are independent units that collect information in the field and report directly to BAIS headquarters and the intelligence units that are an organic part of the territorial command structure. All military intelligence reporting converges at the top of the military hierarchy, the armed forces commander.

BIN conducts intelligence operations (with support from TNI intelligence personnel) and collection and analytical tasks. The BIN chief is

---

[1] Kyrway, 2000; Ingo, 2000; discussions with BAIS and BIN personnel, Jakarta, February 2002.

[2] His name is also spelled *Murdani,* but his personal preference is Moerdani.

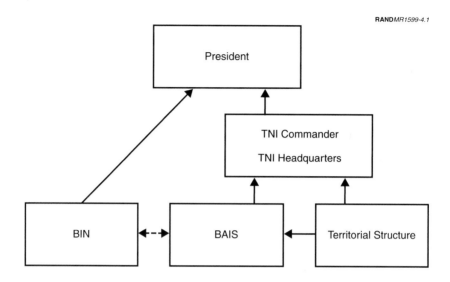

RAND*MR1599-4.1*

Figure 4.1—Structure of Indonesian Intelligence Community

also the president's chief intelligence adviser. The organization has its own domestic and foreign intelligence network, and collects and reports on political, economic, social, cultural, ideological, security, and defense matters including, of course, problems of international and domestic terrorism and subversion. There is no direct link between the two agencies, although BAIS and BIN officers meet periodically at the staff level and maintain the informal personal relationships that are so important in the Indonesian context.[3]

The failures of Indonesian intelligence in detecting acts of violence or identifying their sources, and suspicions that the intelligence services were pursuing their own agendas, made clear the need to revamp the structure and improve central government control of the agencies.[4] After extensive consultations with the parliament and the

---

[3]Discussions with BAIS and BIN personnel, Jakarta, February 2002 and June 2002.

[4]Air Marshal Hanafie Asnan was quoted as saying that the intelligence system was weak because bombings occur without previous warning or detection, but he wondered whether the bombings occurred because of poor intelligence capabilities or because intelligence personnel were involved (cited in International Crisis Group, 2001d, p. 6).

military, the Wahid government reorganized the intelligence network in 2001. As mentioned earlier, BAKIN was restructured, renamed BIN, and made responsible to the parliament and the president. Procedures were to be established to give the parliament an oversight function over the agency.[5]

Still, although President Megawati elevated the BIN chief, retired lieutenant general Abdullah Mahmud Hendropriyono, to cabinet status, there is no institutional mechanism to coordinate the work of the different intelligence agencies, as there is in the United States. The Indonesian intelligence services also lack the legal authority to control international money flows and take other actions to curb suspected terrorist activities. Indonesian officials recognize the need for strong antiterrorist legislation, but as of June 2002, the required legislation remains at the discussion stage. In an interview with one of the authors of this report, Speaker Amien Rais of the Majelis Permusyawaratan Rakyat (MPR, the People's Consultative Assembly) expressed confidence that the parliament will pass a strong law to enable the authorities to take effective action against terrorism, but cautioned about the need to ensure that the law was not used to suppress political opposition, as had been the case in the Suharto era.[6]

---

[5]The goal of the reorganization, beyond strengthening central control, was to establish a new intelligence paradigm: a shift from the New Order focus on surveillance of internal political affairs to preventative security: "to search for information much earlier so that every potential threat to the nation and state can be detected" (Dewan Perwakilan Rakyat [parliament] Commission I chairman Yasril Ananta Baharuddin, cited in Ingo [2000]).

[6]Interview with Amien Rais, Jakarta, June 2002.

Chapter Five

THE CHANGING POLITICAL ROLE OF THE MILITARY

THE MILITARY UNDER SUHARTO

Until September 30, 1965, two forces stood in precarious balance in President Sukarno's so-called guided democracy—the military and the Indonesian Communist Party (PKI), then the third-largest communist party in the world and an increasingly influential factor in Sukarno's government. Sukarno, Indonesia's founding president, had led the country through a period of unstable parliamentary democracy until 1959, when he discarded the system of checks and balances that had produced a political stalemate and introduced an authoritarian system called "guided democracy." Under this guided democracy, the PKI and its affiliated mass organizations, with Suharto's backing, vastly expanded their membership and influence. The growth of PKI power alarmed other forces in Indonesian society, particularly the Muslim community, but only the army had the power, cohesiveness, and discipline to block what appeared to be the PKI's inexorable march to power.

That delicate balance of power between the military and the PKI was destroyed when six of the most senior members of the general staff were assassinated on the evening of September 30, 1965, in a failed coup led by junior officers under the leadership of the commander of the presidential guard. In the violent anti-Communist backlash that followed, the PKI was destroyed as a political force. The destruction of the PKI left the military as the unchallenged arbiter of Indonesian politics, with Major General Suharto, commander of the strategic reserve and the chief organizer of the opposition to the coup, sitting uneasily at the top of the power structure.

After power was formally transferred to Suharto at the General Session of the Provisional Consultative Assembly in 1968, Suharto and his "brain trust," under the direction of his trusted intelligence assistant Ali Murtopo, began to lay the foundations of the New Order regime. A bureaucracy-based organization, Golkar (an abbreviation for *Golongan Karya,* or "functional groups"), was established as the political instrument of the New Order. The old Sukarnoist political party, the Indonesian National Party (PNI), the Indonesian Socialist Party (PSI), and the Muslim parties were undermined from within and forced to merge into two authorized parties, which evolved into the Indonesian Democratic Party (PDI) and the Muslim United Development Party (PPP) (Noer, 2000).

In the early years of the New Order, the army played a much more overt role in politics than had previously been the case—so much more that some outside observers might have confused the regime with a military dictatorship. Military officers held the key positions in the cabinet and in the higher levels of the bureaucracy and were allocated 20 percent of the seats in the legislature.[1] The military tightened its control of local government through the use of the territorial command structure. Territorial commanders, as one senior officer put it, had to wear "the yellow jacket of Golkar."[2] The Kodim commander was harnessed to political duties in the regency, as was the Koramil commander at the subdistrict level and the Babinsa in the village.[3] The practice of seconding military officers to positions in the

---

[1]In 1980, almost 50 percent of the cabinet positions, 75 percent of the posts of secretary-general, 80 percent of the posts of director-general, 84 percent of the posts of minister secretary, and 75 percent of provincial governors' posts were taken up by military officers (Koekebakker, 1994).

[2]Lieutenant General Johny Lumintang, quoted in United States–Indonesia Society (USINDO) (2000), p. 24.

[3]This was the real situation, although no one in authority would admit it. Officially, the military was neutral and its members were not permitted to vote so that they would not become embroiled in politics. Of course, this stance was all a facade. But when Army Chief of Staff Hartono wore a Golkar jacket at a political rally, it was greeted with strong condemnation by Edi Sudrajat and many other retired officers. Appearances were still important, even as late as 1996.

civil administration, known as *kekaryaan*, was expanded.[4] At the same time, a number of institutions, largely staffed by military officers, were established to manage the country's political and social forces.[5] Paradoxically, just as the military's influence increased vis-à-vis other sectors of Indonesian society, it steadily lost much of its room for autonomous action vis-à-vis the president.

Military support for Suharto in the period following the attempted coup was not unconditional. Suharto's consolidation of his personal power and his style of government repeatedly brought him into conflict with his generals. Several of the officers who played key roles in helping Suharto seize power after September 30, 1965, later turned against him (Vatikiotis 1993, p. 18). In the latter stages of the New Order, the power of the military as an autonomous political actor gradually eroded. Suharto built up palace cliques, groups of economic technocrats, and Islamic groups, such as the Indonesian Association of Islamic Intellectuals (ICMI), as counterweights to the military. The number of military officers serving in the cabinet and in the bureaucracy decreased (Koekebakker, 1994). Only four ministers in the 1988 to 1993 cabinet were active duty officers, and the number declined further in the 1993 cabinet (Vatikiotis 1993, p. 25).

In 1993, the military reacted against the downgrading of its position by forcing Suharto to accept one of its own, General Try Sutrisno, as vice president. Departing from the tradition of waiting for Suharto's recommendation, the military faction in the MPR nominated Sutrisno, even though the military was fully aware that Suharto preferred its adversary, B. J. Habibie. To avoid an open rift with the military, Suharto accepted Sutrisno but retaliated by drastically reducing the number of military officers in the new cabinet.

During the latter part of his lengthy reign, Suharto sought to extinguish any independent power centers within the military. General Moerdani wielded great power during his tenure as armed forces commander (1983–1988) and minister of defense and security (1988–

---

[4]This practice allowed Suharto and the military to replace officials suspected of loyalty to Sukarno or the Communist Party with reliable military personnel (Callahan, 1999, p. 12).

[5]Among these institutions were the Special Operations (*Opsus*) the Special Task Force (*Laksus*), and the Security and Order Command (*Kopkamtib*) (Noer, 2000).

1993), but he was not able to prevent his own removal and a large-scale purge of his supporters in 1993. Under one of Moerdani's later successors as armed forces commander, General Feisal Tanjung, there was frequent reshuffling of personnel, each time involving large numbers of senior officers. Loyalty and ties to the president were key factors in assignments and promotions. On one level, these changes accorded with a number of structural requirements, such as the need to correct the imbalance between the number of senior officers and the number of upper-level positions and to expand command opportunities for younger officers. At the same time, the frequent command changes prevented the consolidation of power centers that could challenge Suharto's authority.[6]

THE HABIBIE INTERREGNUM AND THE EAST TIMOR CRISIS

The military was an important actor in the back-room maneuvers that went on in the transition from Suharto to B. J. Habibie and from Habibie to Wahid, but it did not intervene to force an outcome from the power struggles that played out on the streets and in the MPR. In the turbulence that accompanied Suharto's resignation in May 1998, the new president, Habibie, and the military leadership resisted an attempt by Suharto's ambitious son-in-law, then Kostrad commander Lieutenant General Prabowo Subianto, to have himself appointed as armed forces commander in place of the incumbent, General Wiranto. The next crisis came in mid-November 1998, when large student demonstrations called for Habibie's resignation. The students were confronted by vigilantes known as *Pam Swakarsa*, who included Muslim extremists, reportedly organized with military backing to defend the Habibie government.[7]

A technocrat who owed his position entirely to his personal relationship with Suharto, Habibie lacked a power base in either the military

---

[6]See Shiraishi, 1998, and Kammen and Chandra, 1999, pp. 30–40 and 48–53, for an extended discussion of the factors influencing accelerated military rotations in the 1990s. The authors of these documents posit, inter alia, that the necessity of maintaining institutional rationality coincided with President Suharto's interests.

[7]Well-informed sources in Indonesia and abroad maintain that the Pam Swakarsa were sponsored by TNI leaders.

or in Golkar. Nevertheless, without consulting the military or even key members of his cabinet, Habibie decided to hold a referendum on autonomy or independence for East Timor, despite the fact that he did not have the constitutional authority to make such a decision. Habibie's decision was a break with the New Order's policy of refusing to compromise on the issue of sovereignty or to contemplate any special autonomy status for East Timor. That decision set in motion the chain of events that led to the vote for independence, the violent rampage by military-backed pro-Indonesian militias that followed the referendum, the introduction of the Australian-led International Peacekeeping Force for East Timor (INTERFET), and eventual independence of the half-island.[8]

There was little violence or interference with the referendum, held on August 30, 1999, but once the results were announced—a 78.5 percent vote against autonomy within Indonesia, that is, for independence—pro-Indonesian militias and some military units unleashed a destructive campaign of violence. The violent rampage virtually destroyed East Timor's infrastructure, forced a large part of the population to flee to the mountains or to move to the relative safety of West Timor, seriously damaged Indonesia's international reputation, and generated a new round of U.S. sanctions.[9]

A number of theories have been advanced to explain the reasons for the violence. Initially, the Indonesian government claimed that the violence was the natural result of the civil conflict between pro-integrationist and pro-independence East Timorese. In fact, the Indonesians had maintained for years that the East Timorese, fractured into clans and with a history of violence even during the Portuguese colonial era, would set upon each other if the Indonesian army reduced its presence in the province. But this claim is not consistent with the largely one-sided nature of the rampage by the militias. The pro-independence Falintil guerrillas by and large maintained discipline and did not attack the militias, which would

---

[8]The East Timor crisis is analyzed in greater detail in Rabasa and Chalk, 2001, Chapter 3. See also Fox and Soares, 2000. Chapter Eleven of this report discusses the consequences of the violence on East Timor for U.S.–Indonesian relations.

[9]According to press reports, some 190,000 to 300,000 people fled into the mountains during the violence, in addition to 140,000 who fled to West Timor ("International Peacekeepers ...," 1999).

have given credibility to the Indonesian forecast of political and clan violence.

There is no doubt that the violence was carried out with the support of some elements of the Indonesian army, particularly elements of the Army Special Forces Command (Kopassus), which had organized and trained the militias. Some militias dated back to the 1970s, when they were formed to defend their communities against attacks by pro-independence Falintil guerrillas, provide intelligence to the Indonesian military, and serve as auxiliaries in counterinsurgency operations. Others were only formed in early 1999 after the announcement of the referendum. In many cases, the militias were augmented by outsiders, mostly from other islands in Indonesia, but also from as far away as the Jakarta underworld.

One theory posits that the high command was unable to control the behavior of the troops in the field. The then armed forces commander, General Wiranto, appeared to support this theory when he blamed "psychological factors" for the debacle. This suggested that the Indonesian military stationed on East Timor, which included many East Timorese troops, was so committed to keeping the province that it was beyond the control of the high command.

Another theory involves a deliberate conspiracy by the high command to subvert the result of the referendum and keep East Timor in Indonesia, or more plausibly, partition East Timor, with the pro-Indonesian forces retaining the more economically viable areas adjacent to the West Timor border. The military's decision to unleash the violence has also been explained as an object lesson to other provinces that may have secession in mind, or is seen simply as retribution.[10]

---

[10]The analysis of the development of the East Timor crisis described here is based on contemporary press reports and on a discussion at a USINDO Conference on East Timor, Washington, D.C., September 10, 1999, with panelists Donald K. Emmerson, Sidney Jones, R. William Liddle, and Constancio Pinto, and on a seminar on East Timor at the Paul H. Nitze School of Advanced International Studies (SAIS), Washington, D.C., September 22, 1999, with former ambassadors to Indonesia Paul Wolfowitz and Edward Masters and Eliot Cohen, professor of strategic studies at SAIS.

The most likely, but still unproven, explanation is probably a combination of the two theories.[11] The failure of the strategy, if in fact it was a strategy, was made clear in the sequence of developments that led to Jakarta's reluctant acquiescence in the deployment of INTERFET, which meant the effective end of Indonesian rule over East Timor.[12]

Under attack by opposition forces, Habibie was obliged to call for new parliamentary elections. The June 1999 "emergency election" was a watershed event—the first genuinely free election in Indonesia since Sukarno's introduction of guided democracy in the late 1950s, and it resulted in an opposition majority in the parliament. The military, also for the first time since the 1950s, remained neutral in the election. Meeting in October 1999, the MPR rejected Habibie's accountability speech, forcing his resignation, and after some complex maneuvering, elected Abdurrahman Wahid as president.

WAHID'S TENUOUS RELATIONSHIP WITH THE TNI

During his first year in office, President Wahid concentrated on asserting control over the military. General Wiranto was moved from armed forces commander to the position of coordinating minister for political and security affairs, which removed him from the military chain of command. In February 2000, Wahid asserted his authority by dismissing Wiranto. Wiranto's removal also involved the transfer of 74 commanders and staff officers in a reshuffle reminiscent of the Suharto era. The reshuffle included the controversial appointment of Lieutenant General Agus Wirahadikusumah, an outspoken reformer unpopular with other senior officers and a Wahid protégé, to the key position of Kostrad commander. A leading Indonesian analyst thought that Wahid had dismissed Wiranto "to break the myth of Army power."[13] Analysts in Singapore posited that Wahid was simply

---

[11]See Crouch, "The TNI and East Timor Policy," and Haseman, "The Misuse of Military Power and Misplaced Military Pride," in Fox and Soares, 2000, pp. 160–191.

[12]A key political objective—achieving Indonesian acceptance of East Timor's independence—was attained when the MPR voted in October 1999 to accept the result of the referendum. President Wahid visited East Timor on February 29, 2000, and was welcomed as a friend by the East Timorese leadership. East Timor formally became independent on May 20, 2002.

[13]Conversation with Brigadier General (retired) Soedybio, Jakarta, March 2000.

exercising the time-tested divide and conquer methods that Suharto had employed in his time in order to consolidate control of the military. In private discussions, some Indonesian military officers criticized Wahid's role in the reshuffle and argued that the development of healthy civil-military relations was a two-way street that required the civilian political leadership to respect the military's internal decisionmaking process for promotion and assignment.

Wahid's erratic style of governance, a growing perception of government incompetence, and his alienation of members of the coalition that brought him to power led to the erosion of his political base and to his eventual removal from office. In April 2000, Wahid antagonized the two largest parties in the parliament—Vice President Megawati Sukarnoputri's Indonesian Democratic Party–Struggle (PDI–P) and the former ruling party, Golkar—when he dismissed two cabinet ministers, Minister of Investment and State-Owned Enterprises Laksamana Sukardi, a confidant of Vice President Megawati, and Trade Minister Jusuf Kalla, a Golkar supporter, on charges of graft that Wahid was unable to substantiate.

Wahid's deteriorating political standing and loss of parliamentary support in the second half of 2000 also weakened his hand vis-à-vis the military. In August 2000, the People's Consultative Assembly, controlled by the opposition, forced Wahid to agree to share power with Vice President Megawati (a commitment Wahid subsequently failed to honor). Wahid was also forced to replace Wirahadikusumah as Kostrad commander in an effort to placate conservative factions in the TNI. In January 2001, an attempt by Wahid to appoint Lieutenant General Wirahadikusumah to replace General Tyasno Sudarto as army chief of staff failed after 46 army generals threatened to resign.

Wahid's political standing was further weakened in January 2001, when thousands of student demonstrators converged on the parliament to demand his resignation after a parliamentary committee report reprimanded the president for his alleged part in the financial scandals known as "Buloggate," in which funds were allegedly siphoned off from the state logistics agency (Bulog), and "Bruneigate," which involved the disposal of funds donated by the Sultan of Brunei for humanitarian relief in Aceh.

On February 1, 2001, the 38 TNI and police representatives in the parliament joined in the vote to censure Wahid, a step that set in motion the impeachment process that led to the president's removal later in the year. By taking this step, the military laid down a marker that it expects the civilian political leaders to behave responsibly.[14] The military and police parliamentarians abstained on the second Dewan Perwakilan Rakyat (DPR, the People's Representative Council, or House of Representatives) vote in May, but rejoined the majority and voted to remove the president at the Special Session of the MPR in July.[15] Wahid several times attempted but failed to secure the military's support for the declaration of a state of emergency and the dissolution of the parliament. In any event, the military's withdrawal of support for Wahid was certainly a key element in his political downfall.[16]

THE MEGAWATI CONSENSUS

Military support was critical to Megawati's peaceful ascension to the presidency and she has established a much more harmonious relationship with the TNI leadership than her two predecessors had. Megawati's political history would not have suggested the development of a collaborative relationship with the TNI. The military had been instrumental in the removal of her father, Indonesia's founding president Sukarno, from power and had instigated her removal as president of the PDI and the violent attack on her supporters, who had occupied the party headquarters, in July 1996. That said, Megawati's nationalist sentiments and secularist outlook were closer to the military's own ideology than Wahid's traditionalist Islam or Habibie's Islamic/technocratic ideology. As vice president, Megawati

---

[14]In addressing students at the Command and Staff School at Bandung, General Endriartono Sutarto said that political leaders were consumed with attaining power without regard for the consequences for the nation and called on them to put national interests before personal and group interests ("Army Chief Lashes Out ...," 2000).

[15]Technically, the DPR, in accordance with MPR procedures, determined that the president's response to its warning memorandum was unsatisfactory and issued a second memorandum. In May 2001, the DPR judged that Wahid's response to its second memorandum was also unsatisfactory and requested a Special Session of the MPR to hear a statement of presidential accountability. The Special Session of the MPR convened and removed the President in July 2001.

[16]For an analysis of Wahid's downfall, see National Democratic Institute (2001).

took pains to cultivate the support of TNI leaders, reassuring them of her commitment to Indonesia's unity and territorial integrity. Megawati also offered a welcome degree of stability and predictability after Wahid's erratic leadership.

Several retired senior military officers play key roles in Megawati's government—all are associated with the reform camp in the TNI. Their personal ties and influence within the TNI can be expected to facilitate a smoother course of civil-military relations and the progress of military reform.

Coordinating Minister for Security and Political Affairs Susilo Bambang Yudhoyono has the critical tasks of ensuring domestic order and civilian control of the military. Yudhoyono, a retired lieutenant general associated with the reformist camp in the TNI, led a team of 32 senior officers who formulated the new Indonesian military doctrine, the "New Paradigm," that mandates a shift from internal security to external defense (see Chapter Four). Yudhoyono is a politically astute military intellectual who successfully navigated all of the twists and turns of Indonesian military politics since the fall of Suharto.

In 1999, together with General Wiranto, the armed forces commander, Yudhoyono helped to block a bid for power made by Suharto's ambitious son-in-law, Lieutenant General Prabowo Subianto.[17] Yudhoyono was appointed minister of mines and energy in the first Wahid cabinet and replaced Wiranto in the political and security portfolio after the latter's dismissal in 2000. In the crisis leading to the removal of Wahid, Yudhoyono opposed Wahid's threats to dissolve the parliament. Wahid dismissed him and replaced him with Lieutenant General Agum Gumelar, another retired officer with close links to then Vice President Megawati.[18] After she became president, Megawati reappointed Yudhoyono to the powerful security and political affairs post. Yudhoyono's performance in office since his reap-

---

[17]Some analysts doubt that Prabowo was in a position to make a meaningful bid for power in 1999, but the general perception in Indonesia is that Prabowo was maneuvering to replace Wiranto as armed forces commander as a prelude to gaining even greater power.

[18]This move was interpreted as a political gesture by President Wahid to improve his relations with Megawati, in the context of the political maneuvering leading to Wahid's impeachment and removal by the MPR.

pointment has been cautious. He reportedly has been reluctant to crack down openly on Islamic extremists, preferring to work behind the scenes; consequently, he has avoided becoming a target of criticism by Muslim political factions.

Agum Gumelar, a retired three-star general and long-time Megawati supporter and military adviser, entered Megawati's cabinet as minister of transportation, a position he held previously under Wahid. Gumelar was instrumental in Megawati's election to head the PDI in 1993.[19] In 1996, Gumelar openly defended Megawati after Suharto engineered her removal from the PDI leadership. Gumelar is also reputed to have a strong personal base of support within the TNI.

Abdullah Mahmud Hendropriyono, director of the reorganized state intelligence agency, BIN, also a retired lieutenant general, is an equally important ally of the president. He served as minister of transmigration under President Habibie. Elevated by Megawati to cabinet rank as BIN chief, Hendropriyono is a key player in helping Megawati contain the security threats unleashed by the upsurge of Muslim militancy in response to the war on terrorism and the U.S. military campaign in Afghanistan. Hendropriyono served for 20 years, from his graduation from the military academy in 1967 to 1986, as a Kopassus and intelligence officer. He served as a directorate chief in BAIS and then was appointed commander of the Jakarta Kodam. Remarkably popular with the Jakarta populace, he apparently garnered too much good publicity and fell out of favor with Suharto.[20]

Hendropriyono is close to Megawati and is one of her principal military advisers. His standing with Megawati dates to 1993, when he and Gumelar were in the Indonesian intelligence agency and vetted her nomination for PDI party leader, which allowed her to ascend to the chairmanship of the PDI in 1993. Hendropriyono is reputed to be *the* member of the Megawati administration most willing to take on

---

[19] For discussion of the military's role in Megawati's election at the 1993 PDI Congress see PPW-LIPI Research Team (1999, pp. 156–157).

[20] According to Tapol, the Indonesian human rights campaign, Hendropriyono maintained a high profile and made himself popular by making tough statements about cracking down on crime. This worried Suharto, who had an aversion to popular officers whom he saw as a threat to his power (Tapol, 2001).

the threat of terrorism and Islamic extremism and, as a result, has come under attack by some Muslim political groups.[21]

Another senior general in Megawati's cabinet is the minister of interior, retired lieutenant general Hari Sabarno. He previously headed the TNI and police faction in the parliament and assisted Megawati's rise to power. The ministry of interior is responsible for supervising regional governments and the decentralization process.

The presence of influential retired senior officers in the cabinet helped to cement a strong relationship between Megawati and the military, which will be critical for Indonesia to navigate the multiple security challenges posed by the presence of groups linked to international terrorist networks, Islamic radicals, separatism in Aceh and Papua, and the other centrifugal forces at work in the archipelago.

Tensions resurfaced at the end of 2001 over the prospective replacement of the armed forces commander (Panglima), Admiral Widodo, who had served in that position well beyond his mandatory retirement age. With the 2004 elections approaching, the selection of the Panglima assumes great political importance ("Indonesia's Military Power Play," 2001). Some army sectors opposed Widodo's replacement (not because of any support for Widodo, but because of disagreements over who should replace him and over other military appointments). These disagreements forced Widodo's extension as Panglima until June 2002, when he was replaced in that position by the former army commander, General Endriartono Sutarto.[22]

---

[21]The tension between Hendropriyono and some human rights and Muslim groups dates to his role as the local TNI commander in the suppression of a radical Muslim sect in Lampung, Sumatra. The details of the event are a matter of controversy. According to Hendropriyono, he was obliged to use force after sect members killed one of his officers.

[22]There were different possible reasons for the delay in replacing Widodo. One was the issue of whether the Panglima position should be rotated among the services, as intended by former president Wahid. Another was competition among senior generals over who should replace Sutarto as army commander. A third issue was whether the president should be bound by the list proposed by the TNI Promotion Council (Wanjakti) or whether she could go outside of the Wanjakti process to select the next commander. (See "Terjadi Pembangkangan ...," 2001.) As it turned out, Sutarto's selection met the requirement that the armed forces commander should have previously served as chief of staff of one of the services.

CIVIL-MILITARY RELATIONS IN THE NEW DEMOCRATIC ORDER

The multiple crises that accompanied the fall of Suharto prompted a reexamination of the military's role in politics. The TNI responded to the pressures for change by retreating from its political role and undertaking a revision of the doctrine. The most important potential development was the TNI's formal abandonment of its dual function—the linchpin of the military's involvement in political affairs. Under the new dispensation, the military is still regarded as having a sociopolitical function, but that function is no longer viewed as being separate from defense. Emblematic of this change was the abolition of the chief of staff for sociopolitical affairs position in 1998. The last incumbent to that position was Lieutenant General Susilo Bambang Yudhoyono, a leading architect of the change, who then moved to the newly established position of chief of staff for territorial affairs.[23]

The Military and Parliament

The most visible symbol of a continued TNI role in the practical political affairs of the country is the military's bloc of seats in parliament. Until the mid-1990s, the military held 100 seats in the DPR. After the fall of Suharto, the military and police representation was reduced from 75 to 38 and was scheduled to be phased out of the DPR and the regional parliaments by 2004, and out of the MPR, which elects the president, no later than 2009, per MPR Decree 7 of 2000. More recently, in the constitutional reforms of August 2002, the MPR voted to move up the date of the phasing out of the military and police representation in the MPR to 2004.

Though reduced in numbers, the military bloc operates under military instruction and votes as a unit. The link between the parliamentary bloc and the TNI headquarters for many years was through the chief of staff for sociopolitical affairs, changed to chief of staff for territorial affairs in 1999, and downgraded to assistant for territorial affairs in 2001. In December 2001, TNI Chief of Staff for Territorial Affairs Lieutenant General Agus Widjojo was reassigned from his post to become the deputy speaker of the MPR. The tie between the

---

[23]That position has now been abolished.

army, the territorial system, and the parliament could not have been more obvious. The role of the TNI and police faction is to ensure that military and security aspects of proposed legislation are considered, and to promote national development and national unity (Lowry, 1996, p. 186).

With the abolition of military and police representation in the legislature, a decision must be made about the political rights of military personnel. Will military personnel be given the right to vote in exchange for relinquishing the 38-seat bloc in parliament? In sheer numbers (approximately 308,000), the strength of the military does not justify so many seats compared with the number of people in the various legislative constituencies. On the other hand, if given the vote, an organized and disciplined military bloc could be expected to exert considerable influence in future elections (Haseman, 2001, pp. 24–26). In Thailand, for instance, every national election presents the unsettling spectacle of entire military units voting en masse according to orders given by unit commanders through the military chain of command and, presumably, dominating the vote tally in the constituencies in which military bases are stationed.

Another significant development in the post-Suharto era is the beginning of effective legislative oversight of military affairs. The DPR, for the most part nothing more than a "rubber stamp" under Suharto, has begun to assert its authority to approve the appointment and dismissal of the armed forces commander and the national police chief and to approve annual budgets. President Wahid's controversial dismissal of police chief Surojo Bimantoro without DPR concurrence at the height of the political crisis in July 2001 was the catalyst for the DPR's decision to bring forward a special session of the MPR to remove Wahid from office.[24]

---

[24](See "Bimantoro's Insubordination ...," 2001, and "MPR Team Agrees ...," 2001.) According to former defense minister Juwono Sudarsono, Wahid's dismissal of Bimantoro turned the military against the president because they feared that the dismissal threatened a split in the police that could be replicated in the army ("The Puppet President," 2001).

"Civilianization" of the Public Administration

Individuals with military backgrounds continue to serve in the Indonesian cabinet and other civilian government positions, but active-duty officers are now required to retire before being allowed to serve in those positions. In years past, active-duty military officers served routinely as cabinet ministers, directors-general within cabinet departments, provincial governors, mayors, regency heads, and in hundreds of positions in the secondary tiers of national and provincial government. Political reform has turned many of these positions into elected rather than appointed positions, which will dilute the national government's influence over provincial and local government. Retired military personnel are eligible to fill almost all of these posts, but must now compete within a much-changed political environment. The requirement to run for popular election, for example, could prove a daunting and humbling experience for retired officers used to automatic appointment in the past.

No More "Practical Politics"

Jettisoning the dwifungsi policy in favor of the New Paradigm fulfills the TNI leadership's strong desire to remove itself from practical politics. Another reform well underway is the TNI's withdrawal from day-to-day practical politics. No longer will senior military officers don the colored jackets of major political parties, as was the case when the armed forces were a key part of the Golkar political organization. At least as important as formal changes are changes in attitudes. Many officers in the past expressed frustration and resentment that they were required to carry out acts designed specifically to bolster Suharto's personal powers or that of his widely despised children or business cronies. Strong-arm tactics by the military, intimidation, intelligence investigations of political opponents, and tight controls on politics were routinely employed to maintain Suharto's control.

The new doctrine and changes in civil-military relations since the fall of Suharto make it less likely that any president can co-opt the TNI for personal political gain. However, although the military as an institution has removed itself from such unsavory practices, it is increasingly obvious that individuals within the armed forces continue to be involved in political manipulation. Elements of the military, apparently acting in response to bonds of personal loyalty and orders outside the institutional chain of command, have been accused of involvement in all sorts of skullduggery throughout Indonesia. As in cases of alleged civilian malpractice, however, conclusive evidence is seldom proffered and impartial investigations are few and far between.

Civilian Ministers of Defense

For the first time since the 1950s, civilians have been appointed ministers of defense—a position hitherto reserved for active duty or recently retired army officers. President B. J. Habibie appointed Indonesia's first civilian minister of defense, Dr. Juwono Sudarsono, in 1998. He was succeeded in that position in August 2000 by another civilian, Professor Mohammed Mahfud, who in turn was succeeded by Matori Abdul Djalil, the former head of Wahid's political party (the PKB), when he was appointed to the Megawati cabinet in August 2001. While this turnover had substantial symbolic importance, it was largely a cosmetic political change because, in the Indonesian system, the military chain of command runs from the president directly to the armed forces commander, who is also a cabinet member. Thus, the locus of military decisionmaking authority remains in the TNI general staff, which remains independent of the Indonesian Department of Defense (Departemen Pertahanan, or Dephan) and is directly responsible to the president through the armed forces commander. This arrangement leaves the Dephan with no command authority over the TNI.

The Department of Defense is charged with programming and budget, national defense policy, and preparation of common doctrine. The minister of defense is thus not in the operational chain of command and does not have the authority to direct the tactical or territorial forces. Nevertheless, there have been recent studies on the possibility of establishing a U.S.–style system that would give command responsibility to the minister of defense. Such a significant change is likely to be many years away, however. During his tenure, Juwono tried to put in place a plan to reaffirm the department's role as the overarching defense policymaking body and to make the armed forces commander answerable to the minister of defense by

2010. Needless to say, little progress was registered in this direction. The 2002 defense law leaves the existing structure very much in place.[25]

Juwono also wanted to revamp and integrate the defense planning and procurement function, currently done independently by each of the services, and to move TNI financing from informal sources to the official budget, currently less than 1 percent of Indonesia's gross domestic product (GDP). Accomplishing this goal, in Juwono's view, would require an annual GDP growth of 6 percent.[26] (See Chapter Seven.) Beyond institutional weaknesses, Dephan is handicapped by the lack of defense expertise of the last two civilian incumbents.[27]

Despite the many political changes that have occurred in Indonesia since the downfall of Suharto in May 1998, there is one constant. The Indonesian armed forces, despite their formal withdrawal from politics, remain the most important and powerful institution in Indonesian society. As one well-informed political analyst summed up: "[The TNI] still exercises political influence at national and regional levels and has the capacity, although currently not the intent, to recapture the political heights" (International Crisis Group, 2001d). Implementation of reforms that materially change the military's role in politics will take time and would have to overcome formidable obstacles such as the parlous condition of the state's finances and entrenched military culture. Moreover, as former defense minister Juwono sagely noted, establishing substantive civilian control of the military will require prerequisite reform and strengthening of civilian institutions, especially the political parties.[28]

The military, like other Indonesian institutions, is a reflection of the Indonesian society and its culture and values and will manifest those of that society. A combination of the military's apparently genuine

---

[25]Don McFetridge, former U.S. defense attaché in Jakarta, one of the reviewers of this report, believes that the subordination of the TNI to the Dephan could come sooner rather than later.

[26]Interview with Juwono Sudarsono, Jakarta, February, 2002.

[27]According to a source in the Indonesian defense establishment, senior government officials routinely go to the TNI chief rather than to the minister when they have questions on defense issues.

[28]Interview with Juwono Sudarsono, Jakarta, February 2002.

interest in reduced political involvement and the maturation of civilian political institutions will be required before real political and military reform becomes a reality. In particular, the appointment of civilians with the requisite depth and breath of defense expertise to senior positions in the Indonesian Department of Defense is a critical prerequisite for the development of effective civilian control of the military. (We summarize this and other goals for reform within the TNI in Chapter Thirteen.)

Chapter Six

INSIDE THE TNI: CAREER PATTERNS, FACTIONALISM, AND MILITARY COHESION

OFFICER RECRUITMENT

As with most military organizations, there are a number of career paths within the Indonesian armed forces that lead to success and promotion to leadership positions. Within the air force and the navy, careers as pilots and ship captains remain the traditional paths to the top ranks. This chapter focuses on the army, which dominates the TNI in size, influence, and number of incumbents in the most senior leadership positions.

The majority of the TNI's most senior officers—of all branches of service—come from the military academy system. All cadets attend the military academy at Magelang for the first year. Army cadets remain there for three more years, while navy and air force cadets move to navy and air force academies at Surabaya and Yogyakarta, respectively.

The military academy experience provides four years of intense bonding among classmates, which continues into significant life-long connections. These class ties become of increasing importance in later assignments so that by the time class cohorts achieve seniority, officers have known each other and worked together for an entire career. Assignments and promotions depend on seniority. Officers who are passed by more junior officers almost never work for those "juniors" again, but classmates frequently work for each other.

The largest source of commissioned officers is the officer candidate school in Bandung, which trains selected senior NCOs. Most officer candidates are in their late 20s or 30s and seldom rise above the rank of lieutenant. The military also supports a nascent university commissioning program similar to America's Reserve Officer Training Corps (ROTC). Professional officers, such as doctors, dentists, and attorneys, come directly from university and incur a military obligation if government funds were used for their education (Lowry, 1996, pp. 117–118). Throughout the history of Indonesia up until the mid-1980s, a military career was considered the best way to reach the top levels of power and, frequently, wealth. The military academy, therefore, was able to attract the cream of the crop of Indonesia's male high-school youths. (Despite plans to enroll women, females have not yet been admitted.) Patron and family relationships are important in gaining admission; those lacking the necessary ties could gain admission through the appropriate distribution of "gifts" to people who are able to influence the admission process. All cadets were subject to a thorough background investigation that screened out political undesirables—usually those with a family connection to the banned PKI and its affiliates.

As Indonesia's economy began to achieve rapid growth in the mid-1980s and beyond, the TNI began to lose the top level of high-school graduates, who changed their perception of the best path to success from the TNI to the business world. Military leaders admitted that the quality of new cadets was lower than in the past, as young people competed for admission to business schools in Indonesia and abroad. Nowadays, the majority of the officer candidates are recruited from what could be considered the rural middle class—families that have some position in their villages, but are not well off by Jakarta standards. Families with TNI connections are the other source of officer candidates. As in the past, there are background checks and close screening of the candidates, the goal being to ensure that the candidates selected will be loyal to the institution. Although regional and ethnic balance is not a stated policy in recruitment, the composition of the classes in fact largely reflects the Indonesian population (see the section "Ethnicity of the Military" later in this chapter).

One step that was taken to attract more top-level students to the military academy was the establishment of the SMA Taruna

Nusantara (senior high school) just outside the military academy campus at Magelang. Well-equipped and well-staffed, the school provides free education and room and board to its students. Open to the top graduates of all Indonesian junior high schools regardless of financial status, SMA Taruna Nusantara quickly became one of the most elite high schools in the country. Matriculation to the military academy was not required, but about one-third of its graduates do opt for a military career (Lowry, 1996, pp. 117–118).

The Indonesian military academy system (*Akmil*) does not grant an academic degree. Much of its curriculum, at all levels, is devoted to intense sociopolitical indoctrination and concentrates on instilling respect for discipline and cohort bonding through very tough and demanding physical training. In recent years, there have been several programs planned to expand the academic curriculum to include granting of degrees, in cooperation with selected universities. For the purpose of international military education exchanges, military educational facilities in most countries (including the United States) give "constructive credit" toward a bachelor's degree for work done in Indonesian military academies when admitting Indonesian officers to U.S. schools.

ARMY CAREER PATTERNS

The standard career pattern for most officers combines assignments in both the territorial forces and tactical forces. Officers are expected to attend a series of schools (see "Military Schools" in this chapter) where important cohort bonding continues. This pattern combines unit command, staff, and territorial assignments designed to prepare each officer for increasing responsibilities that demand knowledge of both traditional military requirements (in tactical units) and Indonesia's unique territorial system (Lowry, 1996, pp. 121).

It was not unusual for some officers to spend their entire careers in the territorial system. While they rarely made it to the rank of general, they often were seconded to civilian government agencies as they neared retirement. Policy generally provided for area specialization in two regions for such officers. Those officers would alternate their assignments between a "good" Kodam on Java or Sumatra and a "hardship" Kodam on Kalimantan or eastern Indonesia. Other officers excelled by remaining in one or both of the major army tactical commands, with only one or perhaps no assignments in the territorial system.

A notional army career pattern could include duty as a combat arms platoon commander immediately after graduation from the military academy, then assignment to a battalion staff in either tactical or territorial units, duty commanding a military district or regional command, tactical battalion command, Kodam staff duty, a tour as an instructor in a staff college or other military school or center, and eventually Kodam command as a major general. A series of notional career patterns is shown in Tables 6.1 and 6.2.

There are also unique assignments available in the military cooperatives and business entities, in the intelligence agencies, and in other specializations that enable some officers to reach a high rank without the variety of assignments that others experience on their way to the senior ranks. For instance, Indonesia's most powerful military officer during most of the 1970s and 1980s was intelligence czar and later armed forces commander General Leonardus Benjamin ("Benny") Moerdani, who spent most of his life in either special forces or intelligence. The best known "special" assignment during the Suharto era was duty as a presidential aide-de-camp (ADC). Suharto had four such ADCs, one from each military service and one from the police. Those officers were carefully selected and were usually of extraordinary ability as well as of proven loyalty and unquestioned discretion. Some "graduates" of presidential ADC assignments in the latter Suharto years included Armed Forces Commander and Vice President Try Sutrisno, Chief of General Staff Sujono, and Armed Forces Commander Wiranto.

Theoretically, assignments are made by separate boards for junior and senior officers. In practice, at the lower ranks, the Assistant for Personnel forwards recommendations to his commanding officer, who reviews those recommendations and sends them to army headquarters for approval. An officer being transferred is normally allowed to recommend a suitable replacement. Given the high levels of class solidarity among members of a military academy class, it is common for an outgoing officer to recommend a classmate to fill the vacancy (Kammen and Chandra, 1999, pp. 43–44). Duties at senior levels invariably combine political factors as well as an individual's professional record and personal connections.

Table 6.1

Notional TNI Standard Career Progression

Rank	Territorial Structure	Tactical Unit	School
Second Lieutenant	Koramil commander	Kostrad or Kopassus platoon/team commander	Officer basic course
First Lieutenant	Koramil commander Kodim staff	Kostrad or Kopassus battalion staff	Branch advanced course
Captain	Kodim or Korem staff	Company/ tactical unit commander	—
Major	Korem or Kodam assistant staff officer	Brigade or higher staff	Student, Army Staff School (Sesko AD)
Lieutenant Colonel	Kodim commander Kodam staff	Battalion commander Brigade/division staff	Student, Sesko AD
Colonel	Korem commander Kodam staff	Division staff Brigade commander Army/TNI staff	Department Head, Sesko AD Student, joint senior service staff college equivalent (Sesko TNI)
Brigadier General	Kodam chief of staff	Army/TNI staff	Student, National Resilience Institute (Lemhannas) Expert staff at Lemhannas
Major General	Kodam commander	Division commander	—

MILITARY SCHOOLS

Virtually all flag-rank officers attend five schools in the course of their careers. The first of these, for army officers, is the branch basic officer course followed, for first lieutenants or captains, by the company commander course taught at the branch school or center. The other services have similar schools at these grades. As a major or lieutenant colonel, the officer will attend the Staff and Command School

Table 6.2

Notional Kostrad/Kopassus Career Progression

Rank	Kostrad	Kopassus	School
Second Lieutenant	Platoon commander	Team leader	Officer basic course
First Lieutenant	Battalion staff	Kopassus staff	—
Captain	Company commander	Tactical unit commander	Command school
Major	Brigade/division staff	Kopassus/BAIS staff	Student, Sesko AD
Lieutenant Colonel	Battalion commander Kostrad/army/TNI staff	Battalion commander Army/TNI staff	Student, Sesko AD —
Colonel	Brigade commander Kostrad/army/TNI staff	Group commander Kopassus/army/ TNI staff	Student, Sesko TNI
Brigadier General	Any assignment	Any assignment	Student, Lemhannas
Major General	Any assignment	Any assignment	—

NOTE: In Kopassus, majors or lieutenant colonels can be battalion commanders, and lieutenant colonels or colonels can be group commanders.

(Sesko). The Army Staff School (Sesko AD) is in Bandung. The Air Force Staff School (Sesko AU) is in Lembang, near Bandung, while the Navy school (Sesko AL) is in Jakarta. Colonels attend the joint senior service staff college equivalent (Sesko TNI) in Bandung. Senior colonels and general officers attend the National Resilience Institute (Lemhannas) in Jakarta, whose student body is drawn half from the military and half from senior civilian government and business leadership. Lemhannas was once an institution in the Ministry of Defense but is now under the presidency of Indonesia.

Each of these five major schools reinforces cohort bonding. At any stage of their careers, most officers can recite the exact current location of their more successful military academy and staff college classmates. As careers advance into more-senior levels, these cohort groups play an increasingly important role in advancing, or stunting, the careers of virtually every officer. The greater the success of members of a particular military academy class in helping to advance the careers of their classmates, the greater the overall success of the class (Kammen and Chandra, 1999, pp. 46–47).[1] Many of the officers who rose to power with General Wiranto graduated from the military academy between 1967 and 1970, while nearly all of the members of the radical reformist "Kelompok 20" group, headed by the late Lieutenant General Agus Wirahadikusumah, were graduates of the 1973 and 1974 classes (Pereira, 2000).

The curriculum at all levels of the military education system places heavy emphasis on indoctrination in the national philosophy, Pancasila, although perhaps not to the same extent as in the Suharto era. As the result, purely military subjects are not covered as extensively or in as much depth as in equivalent Western institutions. The reason, of course, is that the point of Sesko training is less to provide an academic experience than to reinforce solidarity and loyalty to the institution and the nation.

THE PROMOTIONS SYSTEM

Promotions are decided by army promotion boards, whose identity and proceedings are supposed to be (but often are not) highly protected secrets. A large percentage of each military academy class advances at least to the full colonel level. The personnel assignment system plays an important role in this process. Officers often must serve in positions associated with a more senior rank before they can be promoted. This is particularly true at levels below full colonel. Not every officer is promoted with his class, of course. Unfortunate career choices, misbehavior, egregious corruption, and lack of ability can slow promotion. During the Suharto era, some philandering senior officers whose wives were able to gain the ear of Mrs. Suharto suddenly found themselves in dead-end positions.

Some well-placed, well-related, or extraordinarily professional officers are promoted ahead of their classmates. For example, the officer who led the successful recovery of a hijacked Garuda Airlines airplane in Bangkok was advanced to full colonel several years ahead of

---

[1]This phenomenon, of course, is not unique to Indonesia and can be observed in almost every military organization where there is room for military careers to be influenced by membership in military academy classes.

his classmates; another officer who captured East Timor resistance leader Alexander "Xanana" Gusmao was instantly promoted one rank. (All of the members of the task forces involved in the Garuda rescue and the capture of Xanana Gusmao received immediate promotions.)

Barring extraordinarily egregious behavior, however, officers are assured of eventual promotion through a normal career pattern. The TNI does not practice the "up or out" personnel management system familiar to U.S. military personnel. Only at the colonel and general officer levels does the promotion pattern begin to level out as the pyramid of available assignments at each senior rank quickly narrows. Even so, many academy graduates reach at least the brigadier general rank. During the early 1990s, the large and talented class of 1965 eventually saw more than 100 of its members become generals in a rapid succession of assignments. Some of those officers served less than six months before moving to new jobs to allow more classmates an opportunity for key assignments and promotion. (See Table 6.3 for a list of key assignments for lieutenant generals and generals.)

Assignments for major generals are limited to about 25 positions. The most important are the 12 Kodam commands and staff principal positions on the army and TNI staff. Other slots include the commandant positions at the military academy, staff college, and branch centers. The Council on High Ranks and Positions (Dewan Kepangkatan dan Jabatan Tinggi–Wanjakti) makes all decisions on general officer promotions ("Current Data on ...," 2001). Invariably, a number of general officers short of retirement age for whom a "normal" assignment cannot be found are assigned as "expert staff" to both the army chief of staff and the TNI commander in chief.

During the Suharto era, the president himself vetted every promotion list presented to him for approval and frequently made changes in both assignments and promotions. Since then, the TNI has jealously protected its senior promotion system and frequently and publicly criticized "outside interference" in the process on the part of both presidents B. J. Habibie and Abdurrahman Wahid. As can be expected, however, politics will continue to play an important role in general officer promotions.

Table 6.3

Key Assignments for Lieutenant Generals and Generals

Lieutenant Generals	Kostrad Commander
	Army Vice Chief of Staff
	TNI Chief of Staff
	Commandant, Sesko TNI
	Secretary-General, Department of Defense
Generals	Army Chief of Staff
	Armed Forces Commander

Patronage is important throughout the system. Senior officers cultivate personal loyalty and support by mentoring juniors, whose personal obligation to the senior *"bapak"* (literally "father") is afterward deep and long lasting (Lowry, 1996, p. 125). Personnel officers benefit from "gifts" to affix their signatures to assignment orders. The particularly lucrative Kodam slots reportedly command large payments from hopeful candidates. Despite these "traditional" hindrances to a professional quality promotion and assignment system, in recent years the TNI has generally managed to identify and promote to senior levels officers described by outsiders (including foreign military attachés) as professional and highly capable. Many others, of course, bring baggage with them in terms of dubious reputations and political agendas. But, by and large, members of the senior officer corps in the TNI are qualified for their responsibilities.

RELIGIONS OF THE MILITARY

The Indonesian military as an institution has been distrustful of political Islam, partly because the military leadership has been largely dominated by secular nationalists and partly because of the military's experience in suppressing Muslim rebellions in the 1950s and 1960s—a role that accustomed the TNI to viewing political Islam as a threat to the stability of the state. Figures on the religious composition of the TNI are hard to come by, but if a recent Sesko AD class is taken as a representative sample, 12 to 13 percent of the TNI officers are Christians, compared with 8 to 9 percent of the Indonesian population at large. Most Christians are from eastern Indonesia or are Bataks from Sumatra. Based on the same sample, about 20 to 25 percent are *santri* or strict Muslims, and the rest are *abangan* or nominal Muslims.[2]

Although, as just noted, Christians are represented in the TNI in a somewhat higher proportion than in the Indonesian population as a whole, the increasing clout of political Islam throughout Indonesian society, particularly in the aftermath of Suharto's resignation in May 1998, is also reflected in the military. Since Suharto's fall, religious considerations appear to have become more important in military assignments. While religion has been a significant aspect of military assignments for many years, there has been a noticeable resurgence in recent years of "religiously correct" assignments.

The domination of the military by General Moerdani for much of the 1970s and 1980s provides an interesting illustration of the role of religion and its influence on military politics. Moerdani—a charismatic and enormously capable officer—brought Christian officers into important intelligence and command positions in numbers that were far out of proportion to their share of the military's population. For instance, BAIS was heavily staffed by Christian officers, and the Center for Strategic and International Studies (CSIS), an institution with a largely Christian staff, became an important private think tank. When General Moerdani fell from presidential grace—for daring to criticize President Suharto's avaricious children—his successors as armed forces commanders conducted what was popularly known as "de-Benny-ization" of both BAIS and the military command structure. Those identified as "Moerdani men," regardless of religion, found themselves marginalized or given "good assignments" far from headquarters. Never again have non-Moslems had as much influence in the TNI as during the Moerdani era.

While TNI leaders repeatedly claim that neither religion nor ethnicity plays a role in senior promotions and assignments, circumstances during the decade of the 1990s belie that claim. Since 1990, no non-Moslem has risen to a four-star rank in any of the services, nor has a non-Moslem held any of the most significant three-star posts, except for Johny Lumintang's famous 17-hour tenure as Kostrad commander. An extremely capable and politically neutral officer, Lumintang

---

[2]From author's personal data.

was made commander of Kostrad immediately after Suharto's resignation and the new president Habibie's sacking of Suharto son-in-law Prabowo Subianto from that key command. Lumintang was quickly promoted to lieutenant general and assigned to the position, but Muslim generals close to Habibie, led by Feisal Tanjung, and the influential ICMI protested the assignment of a Christian to such an important job. General Lumintang was moved out, to be replaced by an observant Muslim officer, Lieutenant General Djamari Chaniago.[3]

The treatment of non-Muslim officers appears to have improved since the Suharto and the Habibie eras, however. The division in the 1990s of the officer corps into "green" (Muslim) and "*merah putih*" ("white and red" or secularist-nationalist) camps has faded. Christian officers report that their religion no longer clouds their assignment and promotion prospects. A Christian officer was recently assigned to the sensitive position of Director A of BAIS, the first Christian to occupy that position since the time of Moerdani.[4]

ETHNICITY OF THE MILITARY

Ethnicity in Indonesia's armed forces (see Table 6.4) tends to parallel the country's population as a whole, although precise percentages of the various ethnic groups at the senior levels of the TNI do not exactly reflect the percentage of ethnic groups in the country's population.

As can be expected, Javanese—particularly from East Java—dominate across the armed forces. Local recruitment of enlisted soldiers tends to concentrate Javanese in the many units on the island of Java. And they also tend to be well represented in the off-Java units as well, reflecting both the preponderance of Javanese in the Indone-

---

[3]Muslim interests also vetoed the proposed nomination of another Christian officer, Major General Luhut Panjaitan, to the position of Kopassus commander (Pereira, 1999).

[4](From Angel Rabasa's discussions with two general-rank Christian officers.) This is also the view of other TNI senior officers and of independent analysts such as Hadi Soesastro of the Jakarta CSIS, per Rabasa's discussions with Hadi in Jakarta, February 2002.

Table 6.4

Ethnicity of the Military Elite

Ethnic Group	Number of Officers	Percentage of Total
Javanese	25	40
Sundanese	5	8
Madurese	3	5
Balinese	4	6
Batak[a]	5	8
Non-Batak Sumatran[b]	6	10
Sulawesi[c]	4	6
Maluku[d]	3	5
West Timorese	1	2
Unknown	6	10
Total	62	100

SOURCE: "Current Data on the Indonesian Military Elite," 2001, p. 137.

[a]Toba, Mandailing, Karo.

[b]Acehnese, Minangkabau, Palembangese.

[c]Buginese, Banjarese, Gorontalonese, Menadoese.

[d]Ambonese, Talaud.

sian population at large (approximately 60 percent) and their residency throughout the country.[5]

The top leadership echelon is more ethnically diverse than the population at large. Table 6.4 shows that ethnic Javanese fill 25 posts (40 percent); another eight officers are either Sundanese or Madurese. Most of the rest are Sumatran and Balinese. There are very few ethnic Chinese. A Western source with frequent interaction with the TNI knows of only one ethnic Chinese officer.

REFORMERS AND CONSERVATIVES IN THE OFFICER CORPS

There are only a small handful of vocal reformist officers in the TNI today, and they have been sidelined to posts in which they cannot exert significant influence. Similarly, those officers most readily

---

[5]The Sesko AD class cited in the previous section included one ethnic Papuan, two Ambonese (one Christian, one Muslim), and at least one Acehnese. The rest were largely East Javanese, followed by Sundanese, and Minangs and Bataks from Sumatra.

identified as "hard line" or conservative leaders—whether for their political views or their degree of religious zealotry—are also sidelined to nonleadership jobs. The great majority of today's TNI officer corps leans toward moderate reform or neutrality and will follow the orders and policies of the TNI leadership. Moderate reformers include military intellectuals, such as retired lieutenant general Susilo Bambang Yudhoyono, coordinating minister of political and security affairs in the Wahid and Megawati governments, and Lieutenant General Agus Widjojo, and officers with a professional orientation, such as armed forces commander General Endriartono Sutarto, Lieutenant General Djamari Chaniago, and Major General Kiki Syahnakri (Pereira, 2000).

This is not to say that the officer corps is comfortable with the speed (or lack thereof) of military reform. As individuals, senior officers in particular may well lose important perquisites that they enjoyed in the Suharto era. Withdrawal from day-to-day political affairs implies a loss of personal power and the loss of monies paid under the table for political support. The gradual reduction of the army's territorial system will reduce income to commanders at all levels. Better management and transparency in the military's business empire will drastically reduce the leakage of monies from businesses to the military budget and to individual officers. Many of the officers identified as hard-liners are those who oppose, in varying degrees of activity, the loss of those perquisites.

An informal survey of officers at the field level (captains, majors, lieutenant colonels) does not suggest that their attitudes are substantially different from those of their seniors. Most of these middle-rank officers have little interest in scrapping the territorial system. Many of them run small businesses or work at second jobs to supplement their income.[6] For the most part, they look forward to reaching senior officer ranks and the perquisites and economic opportunities that go with those positions. Even those who recognize the need for reform feel discouraged by the enormous inertia of the system and the risk to their careers if their opinions were viewed as a threat to the system.

---

[6]A major makes the equivalent of US$120 a month, including family and other allowances.

SOLIDARITY OF THE ARMED FORCES: UNITY OR FACTIONALISM?

The TNI works very hard to instill in its officer corps a high level of unity and discipline. These characteristics are inculcated through a process of cohort bonding from the military academy through a sequence of schools at the company grade, field grade, and in the general officer ranks, as described earlier in the section on military schools. Also important is the constant use of indoctrination and propaganda to emphasize the storied history of the armed forces in fighting for and preserving Indonesia's independence and national unity (Lowry, 1996, p. 121). This indoctrination serves to contrast the solidarity of the armed forces with the country's history of divisive political leadership. The Indonesian military officer corps is taught from the very first that the TNI as an institution is the foundation and guardian of national unity, a role that can only be carried out through unity in purpose and disciplined application of leadership.

The key analytical question is whether there are cracks in the solid front that the TNI strives to portray to the world that might destabilize the institution. Up to now, the armed forces have maintained their unity and solidarity throughout the post-Suharto political transition. Despite stresses on the institution, the military appears to be in no danger of fragmenting into competing factions. Nevertheless, senior military officers are torn between loyalty to their own seniors, loyalty to the institution, and loyalty to a new chain of command with inexperienced civilians at the top.

The intense competition of civilian politicians—a major change from the political culture of the New Order—also affects the military leadership. Political parties and political leaders actively compete for supporters within the senior TNI ranks. Some were part of the Suharto circle of cronies and family members. Financial incentives to provide sub rosa commitments and support are strong inducements for flexing of military muscles through covert actions that continue to perturb Indonesia's transition to a democratic political order. Many analysts believe that these conditions led to the "rogue elements" accused of a variety of violent disruptions that erupted throughout Indonesia over the past few years (Haseman, 2001, pp.

24–26).[7] Such activities should not be considered as much an effect of military factionalism as of competition by political factions.

The potential for cracks in the TNI's unity comes from not only outside influences but also from fundamental elements of the military culture itself. Junior officers develop personal and professional loyalty to senior officers (bapak) who regularly attempt to identify and cultivate the loyalty of junior officers. Senior officers routinely use part of their income to fund junior officers' education of their children, or the purchase of homes or cars, or the purchase of luxury items not affordable with low military salaries. Acceptance of such favors brings with it obligations of personal loyalty. So, in addition to loyalties to the military institution and classmates and to ethnic and religious communities, a significant number of military officers are also bound by personal loyalties to seniors and to benefactors and business partners outside the military.

---

[7]An excellent discussion of this phenomenon can be found in International Crisis Group, 2000b, p. 16.

Chapter Seven

THE MILITARY'S FUNDING AND ECONOMIC INTERESTS

Discipline, organization, and unity are three important keys to the TNI's strength, both as an institution and as a major player in national politics. A fourth key to its strength is its economic power. The TNI receives only a fraction of its funding from the central government budget. Most of its funds come from off-budget sources that no outside observer has been able to quantify. As Samego et al. (1998a, pp. 25–26) point out, not only does the military require complementary resources for its national defense mission but, in the view of some observers, the military's sociopolitical role requires it to be involved in all fields of public life, including the economy. In fact, much of the TNI's involvement in "politics" centers on its business operations and the huge territorial structure that lends power to those operations.

The military's business empire has important political, economic, and social ramifications. Its involvement in business activities seriously hinders military's professionalization. Moreover, military funding is an important issue in civilian control of the military. Without complete control of the military budget, parliamentary control of the TNI and the police remains fragile. By refusing to adequately resource the TNI, the parliament and the government have abdicated their responsibilities to properly maintain the armed forces and empower those in uniform who distrust civilian over-sight.[1]

The 2002 Indonesian defense budget is about US$800 million, less than 1 percent of Indonesia's GDP and less than 4 percent of the government budget. It is estimated that this amount covers less than one-third of the operational expenses of the armed forces.[2] In fact, the Indonesian central budget has never fully funded the armed forces. The paradox of the New Order was that even though in its early stages it very much had the characteristics of a military regime, the military budget as a percentage of the state budget declined steadily from 27 percent in 1969–1970 to 7 percent in 1993–1994 (Kristiadi, 1999, p. 102). The reason for the military's unwillingness to seek a larger share of the state budget was that by the 1960s a structure of military-run businesses and economic activities was in place that filled the gaps left by the inadequate state budget.

Military business is, of course, not unique to Indonesia. Militaries in many other countries—such as Thailand, Pakistan, and Brazil—in what used to be known as the "developing world" have been heavily involved in economic activities. Only as their economies developed and their militaries became more professionalized did they begin to withdraw from direct participation in the economy. In some Communist and post-Communist societies, the military has been the dominant player in the economy and the main source of skilled business managers.[3] In China, the People's Liberation Army was ordered to withdraw from the business sector in 1998, but the practice

---

[1]Comments by Colonel (retired) Charles D. McFetridge, graduate of the Indonesian Army Command and General Staff School and former U.S. Defense Attaché in Jakarta, June 2002.

[2]Most of the military budget is for personnel and welfare costs. There is an inherent uncertainty in quantifying the Indonesian military's off-budget income, but most estimates concur that it is about two-thirds of total TNI income. Some military sources question this figure and argue that off-budget TNI income is lower than the percentage of TNI income usually cited (interview with Lieutenant General Agus Widjojo, Washington, D.C., February 2002).

[3]In Cuba, military-run enterprises generate 89 percent of exports, 59 percent of tourism revenues, 24 percent of productive service income, 60 percent of hard-currency wholesale transactions, and 66 percent of hard-currency retail sales, and employ 20 percent of state workers (Espinosa and Harding, 2001).

is still prevalent in states such as Cuba and Vietnam (Mulvenon, 2001).

The military's business empire does many things for the TNI. It funds some operational and minor capital requirements, as well as health care, schools, and the type of social services supported in the U.S. military through nonappropriated funds. It provides a social safety net and supplements the abysmally low salaries of its personnel, from junior enlisted men to its most senior officers.[4] The military, therefore, has little choice but to protect this resource. It will take many years for Indonesia to generate a modern system of taxation that will adequately fund its government operations. Until then, the TNI will not give up one rupiah from its off-budget sources that it does not have to surrender.

The Indonesian military's involvement in the economy, as already noted earlier, was consistent with common practice in other countries and with the national strategy that stressed territorial defense and self-sufficiency. As Major General Suhardiman stated, "During the war, the military were engaged in business to carry out economic guerrilla war against the occupiers. The aim was to undermine the occupiers' economy and seek funds needed to finance the war and revolution."[5] The armed forces' participation in the economy took a quantum jump in 1957 when Dutch enterprises were nationalized. Military personnel were placed in prominent positions in these enterprises, allowing the military to develop an economic network that it was able to use to generate income in the deteriorating economic climate of the later Sukarno years. The military's economic role expanded again in 1964, when British enterprises were also placed under military supervision, and again in 1965, when some American properties were taken over (McCulloch, 2000, p. 11).

In the period of fiscal retrenchment in the early 1960s, military salaries, never overly generous, began to fall farther to the point that they no longer met even subsistence requirements. As a consequence, commanders bridged the funding gap in various ways.

---

[4]Military equipment purchases, capital and operational expenditures, uniforms, salaries, and certain allowances are covered by the military budget (discussion with Lieutenant General Widjojo, Washington, D.C., February 2002).

[5]Cited in Samego et al., 1998, p. 47.

Military officers assigned to manage state enterprises were ordered to channel enterprise funds to the military directly, in addition to the income diverted to them and to their subordinates (McCulloch, 2000, p. 12). At the local level, the military resorted to a policy of "communal provision." Local units raised their own funds by levying unofficial taxes and becoming involved in myriad commercial activities. To feed and shelter his battalion, Lieutenant Colonel Rudini (later general and army chief of staff) used military trucks to transport commercial products, set up a chicken farm that supplied meat to the troops, and established a discount-price store in the base's cooperative that sold eggs, among other things (Samego et al., 1998a, p. 52).

As commander of the Diponegoro Division in Central Java from 1957 to 1959, Colonel Suharto created a veritable business-military empire. Suharto and his associates set up a number of companies, with capital from two charitable foundations, or *yayasan*, one ostensibly for the economic development of the region and the other for the support of retired military personnel. The scope of these economic activities exceeded the tolerance of the High Command and Suharto was removed from his position and assigned to the armed forces staff college in Bandung (Vatikiotis, 1993, pp. 15–16).

From these beginnings, the military-run businesses developed under the New Order into an extensive structure including natural-resource extraction, finance, real estate, manufacturing, and construction. The military's machinery for mobilizing funds can be illustrated as a pyramid (see Figure 7.1). The top of the pyramid is the official defense budget that, as noted later in this chapter, represents perhaps one-third of the military's overall income (but no one knows for sure). Below the official budget is the income derived from state enterprises. In the next level down are the TNI-run cooperatives and the businesses owned by the military foundations (the yayasan). Like the rest of the Indonesian economy, these businesses have been battered by the 1997–1998 economic crisis. In the tier below are all other sources, including the businesses organized by individual local commanders. These commanders mobilize funds through services or contributions to local businessmen. Fundraising activities at this level are not necessarily known, at least in detail, to the senior army leadership.

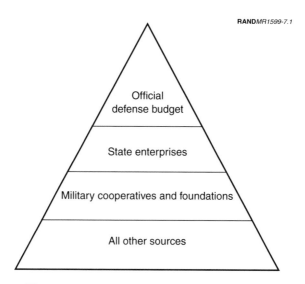

Figure 7.1—TNI Economic Support Structure

The main components of the structure, described here in more detail, include:

1. **State Enterprises.** The expansion of state-owned enterprises came about as the result of the nationalization of Dutch and other Western assets under Sukarno. The most important of these companies for the military are Pertamina, the state oil corporation, and the Badan Urusan Logistik (or *Bulog* for short), the state logistics agency, which controls the distribution of rice and other commodities. There are also large state enterprises operating in the infrastructure (telecommunications and electricity) and banking sectors. In addition to military management or control of state enterprises, retired senior officers were routinely appointed as directors of both public and private firms (Crouch, 1993, pp. 275–282; Samego et al., 1998a, pp. 72–77; McCulloch, 2000, pp. 23–25).

2. **Cooperatives.** The cooperatives function at both the national and local level. They run wholesale distribution businesses that provide affordable basic necessities and relieve operational and personnel costs not covered by the central budget. The structure of the cooperatives is hierarchical. The main level is at the TNI

headquarters. The Kodam (regional headquarters) maintains the central level, and the Korem maintains the primary level. Funding for the cooperatives comes from two sources: member dues and holding companies.

3. **Foundations** *(Yayasan).* The yayasan are chartered as charitable foundations exempt from taxation and also from the law that forbids active-duty military officers from being involved in business activities. The TNI headquarters, army, navy, air force, Kostrad, and Kopassus all have their own yayasan; the Ministry of Defense has two of its own.[6] Each yayasan has at least one and often more holding companies, generally organized as joint ventures with private businessmen, that generate the foundation's income (Crouch, 1993, pp. 282–284; Samego et al., 1998a, pp. 77–79; McCulloch, 2000, pp. 18–23).

ARMY BUSINESS INTERESTS

The army's business network includes the army foundation, the Yayasan Kartika Eka Paksi (YKEP), the main army cooperative (Inkopad), and a primary cooperative (Primkopad). YKEP's business activities are managed by a holding company, PT Tri Usaha Bhakti. The various army interests include the Sudirman Central Business District, which owns 44 hectares in what is known as Jakarta's "Golden Triangle," the Artha Graha Bank, Cigna Indonesia Assurance, Danayasa Artatama (the Hotel Borobudur), other real estate, timber, golf courses, and manufacturing. The foundation is used primarily to provide for soldiers' welfare, especially housing, but it also supports the Army University Ahmad Yani in Bandung, and distributes Muslim New Year and Christmas bonuses to army personnel. Inkopad has business interests that include the Kartika Plaza Group, which owns the Kartika Plaza hotels in Jakarta and Bali, and recreation, construction, fisheries, and forestry businesses. Unlike other sectors of the military's business structure (such as Kopassus)

---

[6]The main military foundations are as follows: Ministry of Defense: Yayasan Sudirman and Yayasan Satya Bhakti Pertiwi; TNI headquarters: Yayasan Manunggal ABRI; army: Yayasan Kartika Eka Paksi; Kostrad: Yayasan Darma Putra Kostrad; Kopassus: Yayasan Korps Baret Merah; air force: Yayasan Adi Upaya; navy: Yayasan Bhumiyamca; and police: Yayasan Brata Bhakti ("Foundations of the Indonesian Military," in Singh, 2001, p. 16).

many of the army's businesses successfully weathered the 1997 to 1998 Asian economic crisis (Samego et. al, 1998a, pp. 79–81; Singh, 2001, pp. 17 and 21; Kristiadi, 1999, p. 104; "Red Beret Business," 2002).

The Kostrad foundation, through its holding company, PT Darma Kencana Sakti, acquired interests in Mandala Airlines, a chemical storage company partially owned by Mitsubishi, a plastic bag company that was a supplier to the state oil company Pertamina, a furniture company, a luxury car importer, and a real estate contractor (Samego et al., 1998a, pp. 82–83; Singh, 2001, pp. 19–20).

Kopassus's Red Berets Welfare Foundation, known by its abbreviation *Kobame*, was founded in 1993 and flourished under the tenure of Suharto's son-in-law Prabowo Subianto when he was Kopassus (and subsequently Kostrad) commander. The foundation teamed up with a private businessman to establish PT Kobame Propertindo. The consortium built the Graha Cijantung, a 55 billion rupiah commercial real estate project, on land belonging to the Jakarta military command. Halfway through the project, the private-sector partner resigned his interests and the business became wholly owned by the Red Berets. However, the interest rate on the bank debt incurred by the project rose above 70 percent as Indonesia suffered the effects of the Asian economic crisis and the project became insolvent. The project's debts were assumed by the Indonesian Bank Restructuring Agency and as of this writing are awaiting disposal. Kobame also set up a shipping business—KMP Tribuana Antar Nusa—but it failed in the economic crisis. Another subsidiary, Kobame Super Sentra, which was in the wholesale business, also went bankrupt ("Red Beret Business," 2002).

NAVY BUSINESS INTERESTS

The Navy established the Yayasan Bhumiyamca (Yashbum), a main cooperative (Inkopal), and a primary cooperative (Primkopal). Yashbum owns Admiral Lines (shipping), resorts, and an oil refinery, and has businesses involved in property rental, import-export, cocoa plantations, maritime electronics and telecommunications, a taxi company, and diving services. The foundation operates two orphanages for the children of deceased seamen, provides scholarships for naval personnel, and operates the Hang Tuah school system with approximately 22,000 students on naval bases. The marines, although formally under the navy, successfully ventured into the real estate business with the Plaza Cilandak joint venture in Jakarta (Samego et al., 1998a, p. 83; Singh, 2001, p. 23).

AIR FORCE BUSINESS INTERESTS

The air force's foundation is the Yayasan Adi Upaya, which manages its business interests along with its main cooperative, Inkopau, and its primary cooperative, Primkopau. The foundation owns the Bank Angkasa, together with the National Electricity Company Pension Fund and private investors. The foundation's other interests include golf courses, container services, hotels, and logging, aviation, and aerial photography enterprises. The foundation provides scholarships and health care for air force personnel and has built houses of worship at air force bases (Samego et al., 1998a, p. 84).

POLICE BUSINESS INTERESTS

The national police, a part of the armed forces until 2000, also established its foundation, the Yayasan Brata Bhakti Polri, and cooperatives, Inkoppol and Primkippol. Businesses included the Bimantara office building in central Jakarta, the Yudha Bakti Bank, and a majority interest in the Bhakti Bayangkara insurance company. The proceeds from these ventures are used to improve police barracks and station houses and to provide housing, medical services, and scholarships for police personnel and their families (Samego, et al., 1998a, pp. 85–87; International Crisis Group, 2001a, p. 20).

NONINSTITUTIONAL BUSINESS ACTIVITIES

There is also a large category of profit-seeking activities conducted by retired and active-duty military personnel and their families outside of the official military business network . This range of economic activities encompasses business operations in both the formal and the informal or "gray" economy. The military as an institution is not involved at this level, but individuals and groups of individuals are. An analyst in an independent Jakarta think tank has suggested that the value of military business is greater in the informal sector than it is in the formal one. Informal sector practices include collecting commissions on goods and services produced by business partners; hiring out of military vehicles, aircraft, or ships; selling fuel and spare parts; and selling commodities from military cooperatives to local communities. These practices extend to illegal and sometimes criminal activities on the part of rogue individuals (McCulloch, 2000, pp. 26–32).

Active duty officers were prohibited from engaging in business activities in 1974, and this ban was reiterated several times—for instance, by Defense and Security Minister General Edi Sudrajat during a parliamentary hearing in 1997. In practice, enforcement was lax and in any event the prohibition does not prevent officers' family members from entering into partnerships with (usually) ethnic Chinese businessmen. In addition, the distinction between authorized and prohibited military business practices is difficult to ascertain. A study of Indonesian military business determined that the most successful retired generals in business were those who had developed strong connections to the private sector while on active duty.[7]

THE DEBATE OVER MILITARY SELF-FINANCING

Until the fall of the Suharto regime, the military's involvement in the economy was not a major issue. The thrust of the criticism of the business practices under the New Order was directed at the predatory actions of Suharto, his family, and his cronies, actions from which, it should be mentioned, the military itself was not immune. (In the early 1990s, Suharto's son Sigit Hardjojudanto and his crony Bob Hassan gained control of a majority of the shares in the Kostrad holding company PT Dharma Kencana Sakti. Kostrad did not regain full control until after Suharto's fall [Singh, 2001, pp. 19–20]). With the onset of reformasi, the rationale for the military's involvement in business began to be questioned. Reformers, including senior officers, recognized that the system of military self-financing had a seri-

---

[7]Businesses conducted by military personnel outside of the official framework (foundations, cooperatives, and enterprises) are discussed in Samego et al., 1998a, Chapter 4. The chapter deals primarily with large-scale enterprises run by retired military personnel, e.g., the business empires of former Pertamina CEOs and other senior officers. Private business activity is carried on at all levels of the TNI.

ous downside. It fostered corruption and illegal activities, harmed readiness, created disparities in the compensation of officers with varying access to off-budget funding, eroded ethical standards, permitted unhealthy independence from government budgetary oversight and control, and produced commercial values inconsistent with military professionalism.

The military's involvement in business activities stands as a major roadblock to the TNI's evolution into a modern professional military force. At the same time, it is widely recognized that it would be difficult to wean the military from its economic activities without substantially increasing the defense budget. This, in turn, as former minister Juwono noted, cannot be done without economic recovery.[8]

Given these constraints, there is a school of thought that argues that initially the focus should be on increasing transparency and accountability in the military's economic activities.[9] Some efforts have been made by the post-Suharto governments to address this issue. Criminal Corruption Law 31/1999 includes the money available to the yayasan in the definition of state finance, thus strengthening the authority of the state auditing agency to audit the foundations. The process of auditing the army's business enterprises began in February 2000. The army hired Ernst & Young to audit the 39 companies under the army's foundation. The audit and evaluation were completed in October 2000, but as of this writing the results have not yet been made public ("Kiki Syahnakri: ...," 2002). Achieving transparency will be an uphill battle, however, given the military culture that allows commanders wide discretion in the use of funds raised through business activities and the inadequacy or lack of records.

---

[8]Angel Rabasa's interview with Juwono Sudarsono, Jakarta, February 2002.

[9]The confrontation between the reformist Kostrad commander, Lieutenant General Agus Wirahadikusumah, and TNI conservatives began in fact when Agus instigated an investigation of his predecessor Lieutenant General Djaja Suparman's expenditure of Kostrad funds. Wirahadikusumah was forced out of the Kostrad position and Suparman was cleared of allegations of corruption after an army investigation.

PART II: SECURITY CHALLENGES

Chapter Eight

THE CHALLENGE OF TERRORISM AND RELIGIOUS EXTREMISM

Indonesia confronts security threats from four sources:

1. Cells of international terrorist networks operating in Indonesia

2. Domestic radical Islamic organizations

3. Religious and ethnic conflicts

4. Separatist movements.

There are, of course, linkages between among threats. The nature of these linkages is not always clear and, in fact, represents one of the most challenging analytical issues in the study of Islamic terrorism and extremism in Southeast Asia. Since many of these groups share the same ideological orientation and biases, it has been relatively easy for the international terrorist groups to infiltrate and influence the domestic radical organizations. Nevertheless, while there are varying degrees of overlap, coordination, and cooperation among international terrorist networks and domestic extremists, their agendas and methods are not always identical. The international terrorist networks focus on U.S. and Western targets, while the domestic extremists are driven largely by internal factors and pursue a domestic agenda. The separatists are in a different category altogether. In the case of the Acehnese separatists, a strict adherence to Islam, although a strong element in the Acehnese identity, is not the primary driver of the rebellion.

INTERNATIONAL TERRORIST NETWORKS IN INDONESIA

Indonesia has all of the characteristics that would make it a hospitable environment for the operation of international terrorist networks.[1] It is a sprawling archipelago of over 14,000 islands with porous borders, weak and dysfunctional government and law enforcement institutions, economic distress, rampant lawlessness and communal strife, unrestrained militias, and a political climate that inhibits government repression of extremists. The military reportedly foiled four terrorist attacks in Jakarta, including planned bomb attacks on the U.S. Embassy, the American Club, and the Hotel Indonesia. In August 2001, four Malaysians were arrested for the bombing of Catholic and Protestant churches and the Atrium Plaza shopping mall in central Jakarta. According to police authorities, a group of Malaysian extremist rejoined the jihad forces in the Moluccas, by way of East Kalimantan and Sulawesi, while others moved on to Jakarta ("Osama bin Laden and Indonesia," 2001).

Indication of an Al Qaeda link to Indonesia came as the result of the detention and trial in Spain of eight alleged Al Qaeda members. One of the suspects received military training at a camp in Indonesia and an individual who reportedly worked in the structure of the Laskar Jihad organization was named as his contact. The training camp mentioned in reports on the trial of Al Qaeda members in Spain was apparently a camp run by a Mujahidin group near Poso, in central Sulawesi, an area that was the scene of violent communal strife from 2000 to early 2002.[2]

Other linkages between Indonesian extremist groups and international terrorist networks came to the surface as the result of the arrest in Malaysia and Singapore of members of terrorist networks associ-

---

[1] The discussion in this section of international terrorist networks in Southeast Asia and the subsequent section on domestic radical Islamic gangs and militias is based on discussions with security officials in Indonesia, Malaysia, and Singapore in February, May, and June 2002, and on extensive coverage in the regional media of the arrests of alleged terrorists.

[2] The camp was abandoned around July 2001. According to a report in *The Jakarta Post*, the camp functioned with about 50 new recruits coming every two or three months. Automatic weapons were available in the camp, but their storage and distribution were kept under the supervision of "men who spoke Arabic" ("Looking for SE Asia's Own …," 2002).

ated with the Jemaah Islamiyah, a group linked to the Al Qaeda network.[3] The goal of the organization, inspired by Wahhabi teachings, was to establish an Islamic state, Negara Islam, encompassing Indonesia, Malaysia, and the Muslim areas of the Philippines. The two key figures in this regional network are both Indonesian clerics, Abubakar Ba'asyir and Riduan Isamuddin, alias Hambali. In the late 1970s, Ba'asyir helped another Islamic figure, Abdullah Sungkar, establish an Islamic boarding school, or *pesantren*, in Ngukri, central Java, which subsequently became the training ground for suspected terrorists.[4] From 1978 to 1982, Ba'asyir and Sungkar were imprisoned by the Suharto government for refusing to acknowledge the primacy of the state philosophy of Pancasila. The two subsequently moved to Malaysia, where Ba'asyir became an expert in *dakwah* (Islamic teaching) and, together with Hambali and Sungkar, set up the Jemaah Islamiyah organization.

After the fall of Suharto, Ba'asyir and Sungkar returned to Indonesia (Sungkar died soon thereafter) and Ba'asyir resumed his politico-religious activities. Hambali's whereabouts are unknown. Malaysian authorities cited Ba'asyir as a key member of the Kumpulan Militant Malaysia (KMM), a group linked to Jemaah Islamiyah and Al Qaeda, after the June 2001 arrest of KMM members in Malaysia.[5] In August 2000, Ba'asyir was appointed as the head of the advisory council of the Majelis Mujahidin Indonesia (MMI), a coalition of militant Islamic groups centered in Yogyakarta. Ba'asyir has been questioned

---

[3] A Jemaah Islamiyah leader in Indonesia denied receiving direction from bin Laden, but admitted to a "sense of Islamic solidarity" with bin Laden. According to a *Straits Times* source, over the past five years, Jemaah Islamiyah received 1.35 billion rupiah (US$135,000 at the January 2001 exchange rate) from the Al Qaeda organization. Indonesian intelligence believes that the amount is even higher. (See "Is There an Al-Qaeda connection ...," 2002.)

[4] Fathur Rohman al-Ghozi, the Indonesian bomb-making expert alleged to be a member of Jemaah Islamiyah arrested in the Philippines, studied at the Ngukri pesantren from 1982 to 1989. He is believed to be the individual known by the code name "Mike," who helped the Singaporean Jemaah Islamiyah cell stake out U.S. targets in Singapore.

[5] Ba'asyir was said to be one of three leaders of the KMM and the Singapore Jemaah Islamiyah group. Among the detained KMM militants in Malaysia was another Indonesian cleric, Mohamad Iqbal A. Rahman (better known as Abu Jibril), a native of Lombok in West Nusa Tenggara. Abu Jibril is believed to have played a key role in arranging meetings between Al Qaeda representatives and Indonesian militant groups such as Laskar Jihad. He was also accused of masterminding bombings in Jakarta.

by the Indonesian police, but denies any involvement in terrorism. According to Indonesian intelligence, the MMI gives political direction to an armed group, the Laskar Jundullah, one of the militias waging jihad in the Moluccas and Sulawesi.[6]

DOMESTIC EXTREMISTS

Although they share the terrorists' vision of an Islamic state, the Islamic gangs and militias (laskar) and radical Islamic political organizations in Indonesia differ from the terrorists in that they are homegrown and the product of very specific Indonesian circumstances. For the most part, the domestic radicals operate in the open. Laskar Jihad has an office in Jakarta and its supporters can be seen soliciting donations outside mosques on Fridays. Their activities are confined to Indonesia, although they do have links to extremists in other countries and receive funding and training from abroad. And although they are anti-American and anti-Western in orientation, by and large they have not directed their attacks against American and Western citizens or interests. That said, the efforts of Osama bin Laden and his network to cultivate radical Muslim groups in Southeast Asia have strengthened and radicalized these groups and increased their potential to destabilize regional governments.

The resurgence of militant Islam in Indonesia had its origins in the latter years of the Suharto era, when Suharto sought to mobilize support among Muslims by presenting himself as a defender of Islamic interests. For most of the New Order, political Islam was labeled as the "extreme right" by the government, ranking just below the communists—the "extreme left," in the hierarchy of political threats. Muslim political activists were persecuted. But in the late 1980s Suharto began to cultivate Muslims as a countervailing force to the military. The wearing of the *jilbab,* or Islamic head covering, by female students in the state schools was legalized. A bill was presented to parliament regulating the Islamic courts and a new marriage law made interfaith marriages practically impossible (Pereira, 1998).

Suharto's most visible step in cultivating support from Muslims was his highly publicized *Haj,* or pilgrimage, to Mecca in June 1991.

---

[6]Discussion with Indonesian intelligence officials, Jakarta, February 2002.

Through one of his foundations, Yayasan Amal Bhakti Muslimin Pancasila, Suharto assisted the construction and maintenance of thousands of mosques and Muslim boarding schools. He also supported the formation of a Muslim think tank, the ICMI, under the auspices of Minister for Research and Technology, and later president, B. J. Habibie. Suharto's son-in-law, Prabowo Subianto, was instrumental in building a support base among Muslim clerics called KISDI (Committee of Solidarity with the Muslim World), which sponsored activities in support of the Bosnian Muslims. Funds were raised through the National Committee for Solidarity with the Bosnian Muslims, chaired by Probosutedjo, Suharto's stepbrother.[7]

The formation of militant Muslim groups accelerated under the interim presidency of Habibie, who sought to mobilize Muslim support in his ultimately unsuccessful effort to retain power. Some of these groups had their origin in the Pam Swakarsa (Self-Help Security Guards), organized by military sectors to confront antigovernment students in the period leading to the special session of the People's Consultative Assembly in November 1998. Among these militant Muslim groups were the Laskar Jihad, the military arm of the Ahlul Sunnah Wal-Jamaah Communication Forum, the Islam Defenders Front (Front Pembela Islam or FPI), the Hizbullah Task Force, the Islamic Youth Front, and other groups.

Laskar Jihad, the best known of these groups, recruits Muslim militants to wage *jihad* (holy war) in the Moluccas and Sulawesi. The commander of Laskar Jihad is Ja'afar Umar Thalib, a 40-year-old Islamic preacher who believes Indonesian Muslims are required to defend Islam against unbelievers by means of jihad. Ja'afar is the grandson of a Yemeni trader who settled in East Java. In 1986, he traveled to Pakistan for Islamic studies and attended a training camp that reportedly included Afghans, Pakistanis, Egyptians, Burmese, Sudanese, Thais, and Filipinos. When the Soviets left Afghanistan in 1989, Ja'afar returned to Java. According to the Indonesian analyst George Aditjondro, many of the leaders of Laskar Jihad, including Thalib, are adherents of the Wahhabi school of Islam. Many of these militants found support in the Tarbiyah movement, which formed

---

[7]The funds raised apparently disappeared into the bank accounts of Suharto cronies. (See Aditjondro, 2001.)

jamaah salaf (congregations) in several Indonesian universities, such as the Bandung Institute of Technology.[8]

Laskar Jihad found a rallying cause in the communal conflict in the Moluccas that pitted Muslims against Christians. The clashes radicalized Muslim opinion in Java. On January 7, 2000, 22 Islamic militant organizations, including Laskar Jihad, staged a rally of more than 100,000 people in the National Monument Park in Central Jakarta, calling for a jihad in the Moluccas. There were allegations that the jihad forces were supported by former Suharto associates and by factions in the security forces. These allegations are unproven, but the fact is that several hundred jihadists received military training (reportedly from Kopassus personnel) in a camp near Bogor, in West Java,[9] and that despite President Wahid's orders to stop them, they were allowed to travel across Java from Bogor to Surabaya and sail unmolested with their armaments to Ambon ("Osama bin Laden and Indonesia," 2001).

Although Laskar Jihad's focus is largely domestic, it maintained informal links with Al Qaeda and some of its associated networks (at

---

[8]The finances of Laskar Jihad are murky. Sympathetic sources say that the organization raises its funds from donations by religious Muslims at the mosques. According to a less sympathetic source, it received funding from one of Suharto's charitable foundations, *Yayasan Amal Bhakti Muslim Pancasila* ("Osama bin Laden and Indonesia," 2001).

[9]The allegations of Kopassus having trained the Laskar Jihad come from discussions with well-informed sources in Indonesia and abroad. However, in correspondence with the authors, TNI historian Ken Conboy questioned the accuracy of these allegations. He pointed out that (1) Kopassus had been making an effort to put on a good face after the bad press it received during the Prabowo era. Conboy found it unlikely that Kopassus would have been conducting a controversial operation that could have earned it more bad press, especially with the government publicly opposed to Laskar Jihad. (2) The Bogor site was too public. Not only was it close to Jakarta, extremists allowed cameras into the compound. If Kopassus personnel were there, they probably would have been exposed. (3) There was no need to use Kopassus. The training given to the extremists was rudimentary, and using an elite force to give such basic instruction was unnecessary. (4) Kopassus was a lighting rod for all kinds of alleged covert operations during that time, but very few of those allegations were supported with solid evidence. Moreover, if the allegations were true, evidence to support them probably would have emerged by now. (5) Of all the TNI elements that have been battling the extremists in Ambon, Kopassus has been among the most effective in countering the Laskar Jihad. As such, the Laskar Jihad could have exposed the hypocrisy of having the same organization that trained them now being used against them. Conboy noted, however, that Laskar Jihad trainers could have claimed some past affiliation with Kopassus, whether it was true or not.

least before September 11, 2001). After September 11, Laskar Jihad leader Ja'afar tried to distance his organization from Al Qaeda. He criticized bin Laden and told the press that he turned down an offer of money and training from bin Laden's representatives. In fact, there were reports of Al Qaeda trainers with Laskar Jihad and of arms shipments from Abu Sayyaf, the notorious Philippine terrorist group (Pereira, 2002, p. 35). After being allowed to operate unmolested for two years, Ja'afar was detained by the authorities in May 2002 on charges of inciting religious hatred and presiding over an illegal execution in accordance with Islamic law (See Chapter Nine).

The Islam Defenders Front, founded in August 1998 by preachers of Arab descent, claims to have ten million members in branches in 16 provinces, but it actually seems to be little more than an extortion racket. Front activities were believed to be funded, at least initially, by political sponsors, but increasingly the front has been involved in extorting protection money from entertainment centers in Jakarta and West Java.[10]

MODERATES AND RADICALS

The dividing line between Muslim moderates and radicals goes to the fundamental question at the root of Indonesia's foundation as a nation state: whether it should be a secular state or an Islamic one. Despite the upsurge of a radical and violent strain of Islam in Indonesia after the fall of Suharto, the large majority of Indonesian Muslims do not support the establishment of an Islamic state. The last parliamentary elections, in June 1999, gave the secular and moderate Muslim parties a large majority in the parliament—the two largest secular parties, PDI-P and Golkar, combined received 57 percent of the votes (USINDO, 1999).[11]

The largest Muslim social welfare organizations in the country, Nahdlatul Ulama and Muhammadiyah, with claimed memberships

---

[10]The origins of the FPI in the Habibie government–backed Pam Swakarsa vigilante group are well established. Allegations of New Order funding can be found in Aditjondro (2001).

[11]At the August 2002 session of the MPR, an effort by the Muslim parties to incorporate Islam into the constitution (the so-called Jakarta Charter) failed to garner significant support.

of 40 and 30 million people, respectively, accept a state based on the principles of Pancasila (i.e., not specifically Islamic). In November 2001, the heads of the two organizations met and, despite their differences, agreed on a common stand to counter the misuse of Islam by radicals.

The explicitly Muslim political parties constitute a small minority of the parliament and they themselves are divided between those who believe that the possibility of establishing an Islamic state should be discussed and those who believe it should not. One of the Muslim parties, Vice President Hamzah Haz's United Development Party (Partai Persatuan Pembangunan or PPP), split down the middle on this very issue. On the religious extreme, there are two relatively small parties—the Justice Party and the Crescent and Star Party—both of which are based on Islam and both of which reject violence.

Certain groups on the radical fringe could be characterized as being inspired by the Wahhabi tradition, but as the noted moderate Islamic scholar Nurcholish Madjid observed, Wahhabism is very much a minority trend in Indonesian Islam and is stigmatized by the mainstream.[12] Accordingly, the main obstacle to Islamic fundamentalism making inroads in Indonesia comes from the mainstream Muslim groups themselves. However, the government, secular forces, and moderate Muslim leaders have been slow to mobilize this latent source of support to take back control of the political and ideological agenda from the radicals. The danger remains that, absent an effective countervailing effort by moderates, the radicals, albeit a minority of Indonesian Muslims, might be allowed to set the parameters of the political debate and therefore drive Indonesia on the path to religious polarization.

RIDING A TIGER: THE INDONESIAN GOVERNMENT'S RESPONSE TO RADICAL ISLAM

The Megawati government's response to the challenge of Islamic terrorists and radicals has been cautious and hesitant. In contrast to the high-profile crackdowns on terrorist networks in Malaysia, Singapore, and the Philippines, the Indonesian authorities have

---

[12] Discussion with Nurcholish Madjid, Jakarta, February 2002.

avoided taking action against alleged members of terrorist networks or local extremists.

Indonesian officials are sensitive to foreign criticism of insufficient diligence in the war on terrorism. They note that, unlike Malaysia and Singapore, Indonesia lacks the equivalent of those countries' internal security laws, which allow greater latitude in detaining alleged terrorists. Therefore, these officials say, they cannot move against suspects without evidence that would stand up in court and, just as important, in the court of mainstream Muslim public opinion. They note that the political environment in Indonesia, a country that is 90 percent Muslim, is different from that in Singapore (a multi-ethnic society), the Philippines (predominantly Christian with a Muslim minority), or Malaysia (with a Muslim majority, but a strong government). Within these limitations, these officials say, they are doing all they can to cooperate in the war on terrorism—for instance, by sharing intelligence with their neighbors, conducting close surveillance of terrorist suspects, and deporting foreigners accused of having terrorist connections.[13]

While Indonesian officials are quite accurate in their assessment of the sociopolitical conditions that shape their approach to the war on terrorism, the authorities' behavior is also a function of the political weakness of the Megawati government and the upcoming 2004 presidential election. Megawati's Islamic credentials are weak and her parliamentary majority is dependent on the support of the Muslim political parties—the same parties that coalesced to block her election as president in 1999. In the view of informed Indonesian analysts, Megawati and her advisors see great political risks and few advantages in moving against the radicals, even if this frustrates the United States and some of Indonesia's neighbors. That said, some officials do recognize the risks in not confronting the extremists sooner rather than later. As a senior Indonesian government official pointed out in a private discussion, better information operations are

---

[13](Discussion with senior Indonesian security officials, Jakarta, February 2002.) The Indonesian government's approach to the issue also reflects a preference for covert over overt methods. In the eyes of the authorities, informal contacts with members of some radical groups are viewed as a means of keeping track of the activities of other, even more dangerous, groups.

needed. There is no reason, he said, why small radical groups should be allowed to shape public opinion.[14]

---

[14]By the summer of 2002, the Megawati government was showing signs of greater resolve to fight terrorism and extremism. The Indonesian authorities reportedly arrested and turned over to the United States at least two alleged Al Qaeda members, and President Megawati has taken a stronger public stand against religious extremism.

Chapter Nine

COMMUNAL CONFLICT IN EASTERN AND CENTRAL INDONESIA

THE CONFLICT IN THE MOLUCCAS

The upsurge of radical Islam throughout Indonesia is intimately tied to the outbreak of communal conflict in the Moluccas, which subsequently spread to other parts of eastern and central Indonesia. The violence was triggered by an apparently trivial incident, an altercation between a Christian bus driver and two Muslim passengers at the Ambon bus terminal in January 1999. Within hours of the incident, fighting spread throughout the city and then to the nearby islands of Haruku, Saparua, Seram, and Manipa ("Maluku: The Conflict," 2001).

The causes of the conflict are the subject of much controversy. Christians blame Muslim radicals seeking to advance a national Islamic agenda; some Muslims say Christians associated with the PDI-P organization initiated the violence in order to intimidate Muslim voters and improve their party's prospects in the 1999 parliamentary election. Still others believe that the violence was instigated by political and military factions associated with the Suharto regime that were seeking to destabilize the emerging democratic political order.

While political manipulation cannot be discarded as a cause of the violence in the Moluccas, there are deeper reasons for the conflict. In the Dutch colonial period, Christians were the majority in the Moluccas and formed a disproportionate part of the KNIL, the Dutch colonial military force (which was largely despised in Java). The influx of Muslims from other islands changed the ethnic and religious makeup of the region.[1] Historically, there had been long-standing friendly and cooperative relations between Christian and Muslim communities. However, economic competition between indigenous Christians and Muslim migrants generated tensions, particularly as the Muslims, whose educational level improved, began to compete for the jobs within the bureaucracy and in the professions that had historically been the domain of Christians.

From Ambon and nearby islands, the fighting spread to the northern Moluccas. Here the violence was connected to intricate local rivalries and reflected a struggle by local elites over control of the newly established province of North Maluku. A massacre of at least 500 members of the Muslim minority in the Tobelo district of the island of Halmahera in December 1999 provoked calls by Muslims for a jihad in defense of the Muslims of the Moluccas, and paved the way for the arrival of Laskar Jihad fighters five months later.[2]

According to independent observers, Christian militias, supported by sympathizers in the police, had the upper hand in the early stages of the fighting. However, the arrival of Laskar Jihad fighters in May 2000 turned the tide against the Christians.[3] The city of Ambon, formerly the economic hub of the Moluccas, was effectively partitioned, with indigenous Ambonese Christians occupying one end of the town and Muslims the other. Indonesian troops guarded checkpoints on the line of partition, but were unable to control the militias. Legal institutions, such as prosecutors and courts, effectively ceased to function. In the areas under its control, the Laskar Jihad implemented its version of Islamic law. In a notorious March 2001 incident in Ambon, Laskar Jihad leader Ja'afar presided over the stoning to death of a man accused of adultery. Ja'afar was briefly arrested for his role in

---

[1]According to official statistics cited in an ICG report, in 1997 more than 57 percent of the population in Ambon city were Christians, but Muslims were a 59 percent majority in the province as a whole (International Crisis Group, 2002, p. 1).

[2]See Rabasa and Chalk, 2001, p. 44; Alhadar, 2000.

[3]Discussion with Harold Crouch, a leading expert on the Indonesian military and former director of the International Crisis Group Indonesia Project, Jakarta, February 2002.

the execution, but was released after protests by some sectors of the Muslim community.[4]

The initial efforts by the Jakarta government to dampen the violence were ineffective. The military increased its strength in the province at the beginning of 2000 to 17 battalions—close to 10,000 personnel—at the height of the violence. A major problem in the employment of these forces was that military and police units were contaminated by sectarian or local sympathies. The reinforcements from outside the province sometimes identified with the residents of the areas they were defending and took their side in the conflict, or just stood by when they were outnumbered by the often well-armed irregulars (International Crisis Group, 2002, p. 5). There were even reports of confrontations between soldiers and police. Elements from a Kostrad unit and a territorial battalion reportedly supported the Laskar Jihad attack on the police mobile brigade (*Brimob*) headquarters and armory in June 2000 (International Crisis Group, 2002, p. 7).

The TNI's solution was to deploy a combined battalion (army, marines, and air force special operations forces) to Ambon with the personnel rotated so as to prevent the development of inappropriate links with local combatants. The battalion responded aggressively to challenges, primarily by Laskar Jihad, which at the time had the military edge. According to independent observers, the combined unit was successful in reducing the level of the violence, but Muslims accused the troops of siding with the Christians. After a June 2001 incident in which 23 Muslims were killed, Laskar Jihad leader Ja'afar Thalib referred to the combined battalion personnel as "dogs of the Christian Republic of the South Moluccas" and issued a *fatwah,* or Islamic decree, declaring that it was obligatory for Muslims to kill the regional military commander, a Hindu officer from Bali.[5]

Although pressure by Muslims led to a decision by the government in November 2001 to withdraw the unit from Ambon, a high-level se-

---

[4]See International Crisis Group, 2002, pp. 16–17.

[5]The Republic of the South Moluccas was a separatist movement suppressed by the Jakarta government in 1950. Muslims have accused the Moluccan Christian side of having a separatist agenda (International Crisis Group, 2002, p. 13). According to Indonesian Islamic scholars, Ja'afar has no religious authority to issue fatwah.

curity official maintained that the "methodology" of the combined unit would be continued in Ambon.[6]

In June 2002, the government established a "Security Restoration Operations Command" in Maluku under Major General Djoko Santoso, the commander of the Pattimura Kodam. The purpose of the new command was to unify efforts by the security and military forces in the province to put an end to religious conflict. Under the arrangement, Santoso would be assisted by a police brigadier general. In connection with the establishment of the new command, the TNI deployed an airborne battalion of the elite Kostrad to Maluku to join the infantry battalion that was already there ("TNI Accused of ...," 2002).[7] One of the purposes of the new command was to put an end to the clashes between army and police units in the province. A confrontation between Kopassus troops and police in May 2002 left several soldiers and policemen injured ("Djoko Vows ...," 2002).

THE CONFLICT IN POSO

As the intensity of the violence declined in the Moluccas, it exploded in the Central Sulawesi district of Poso at the end of 2001. There had been sectarian clashes in Poso, where the Christians constituted a majority or substantial minority, since 1998. Large-scale violence between the Muslim and Christian communities broke out in April 2000, following a brawl between a Christian and a Muslim youth. In the first stage of the conflict, attacks by Muslims on Christians culminated in killings and destruction of hundreds of Christian homes. Hundreds of Muslims were killed in retaliatory attacks by Christian "Black Bat" raiders in May 2000. In August 2000, the governors of the five provinces in Sulawesi declared a truce, but there was a resurgence of violence in April 2001, when a local court condemned to

---

[6]Private discussion with a senior security official, Jakarta, February 2002. The TNI's view is that the unit was only doing its job.

[7]Technically, the arrangement is inconsistent with laws that place the police in charge of internal security in the absence of a declaration of martial law (since June 2000, the province has been in a state of "civil emergency" that falls short of martial law).

death three Christian commanders accused of involvement in the previous year's violence ("The Conflict in Central Sulawesi," 2001).[8]

The conflict took a new turn in August 2001, when the Laskar Jihad declared a jihad in Poso and began to dispatch hundreds of fighters to the district. The arrival of the Laskar Jihad forces again decisively tilted the balance against the Christians. By the end of November, there were thousands of Muslim paramilitary troops in the district, equipped with AK-47s, grenade and rocket launchers, bulldozers, and tanker trucks. The Laskar Jihad and Muslim irregulars launched a scorched-earth campaign, destroying dozens of Christian villages and pushing 50,000 refugees into the Christian-majority lakeside town of Tentena. The situation stabilized in December, when the national government sent two battalions of soldiers and police (composed predominantly of Christians from northern Sulawesi) to Tentena ("Special Report on Poso ...," 2002).[9] Other troops, presumably Muslims, took over the checkpoints previously manned by Muslim militants.

The authorities' reaction to the violence in Central Sulawesi was passive. By and large, the security forces stood by as the intercommunal violence escalated. Some reported attempts by police to intervene were unsuccessful. There are several explanations for the failure of the authorities to respond more forcefully to the violence. A senior Indonesian security official explained that, until they were reinforced at the end of 2001, the security forces in the district were outnumbered by the irregulars and were unable to enforce the law. There have been suggestions that the authorities believed that intervention could only inflame the problem ("Sulawesi: Actors," 2001). This view parallels the approach favored by the security forces in dealing with these types of conflict—allowing the violence to run its course before moving in to restore order.[10]

---

[8]Christians considered the sentence to be biased, given that no Muslims were tried for their part in the violence ("The Conflict in Central Sulawesi," 2001).

[9]For the Laskar Jihad view, see Ayip Syafruddin (2000). Syafruddin stated plainly that the people in Poso have been divided into two camps—the Muslim camp and the Christian camp. He blamed the Christians for instigating the violence, rejected "half-baked" reconciliation efforts, and declared that in order to find a solution "the sins against Islam must be acknowledged and dealt with."

[10]See Footnote 3 in Chapter Three.

THE SEARCH FOR PEACE IN POSO AND THE MOLUCCAS

The government's approach to the conflict is to try to keep large-scale violence from flaring up again. As in Ambon, the authorities have not tried to suppress the Laskar Jihad and other irregular forces (which government officials admit they cannot do), but rather have sought to mediate an agreement between the combatants. At the end of 2001, Coordinating Minister for Political and Security Affairs Yudhoyono and Coordinating Minister for People's Welfare Yusuf Kalla presided over a negotiation between representatives of the Muslim and Christian sides in the South Sulawesi town of Malino that resulted in an agreement to end the hostilities. According to Minister Yudhoyono, the deployment of TNI troops to Poso was followed by the confiscation and destruction of thousands of home-made weapons.[11]

The Jakarta government sought to apply the format for the Poso peace agreement to the Moluccas. In February 2002, 70 representatives from the Muslim and Christian factions met, again in the town of Malino, with central government representatives and local officials to discuss ways of ending the conflict. The two sides signed an agreement to disarm and end all forms of hostilities. As the authorities acknowledge, however, disarming the militias would be much harder in Maluku than in Poso because the magnitude of the problem is greater, and because in Ambon the armed factions are more deeply rooted in their communities, which rely on those factions for security.[12]

The two Malino agreements dampened the communal conflict in Sulawesi and the Moluccas and created a framework for a return to, if not normality, at least to a state of nonbelligerence. In North Maluku, some of the refugees have begun to return to their homes. However, in Ambon, the Muslim and Christian communities remain segregated and the presence of armed Muslim and Christian militiamen continues to be an element of instability. Laskar Jihad, which justifies its presence in the Moluccas and other parts of eastern and central Indonesia by the continuation of religious conflict, continues to fo-

---

[11]Discussion with Coordinating Minister Yudhoyono, Jakarta, February 2002.

[12]Discussion with Coordinating Minister Yudhoyono, Jakarta, February 2002.

ment anti-Christian activity and to oppose negotiations with the Christian side.[13]

---

[13]An International Crisis Group report lists the many possible beneficiaries of continued tension (see International Crisis Group, 2002, pp. 21–22). An armed attack by the Laskar Jihad on the Christian village of Soya on April 28, 2002, was interpreted as an effort to disrupt the Malino II agreement. This attack was one of the factors in the arrest of Laskar Jihad leader Ja'afar Thalib.

Chapter Ten

SEPARATIST MOVEMENTS IN ACEH AND PAPUA

THE WAR IN ACEH

Most Indonesians view the insurgency in Aceh as the most serious current challenge to the Republic's territorial integrity. The province of Aceh, with four million inhabitants and located at the northern tip of the island of Sumatra, is according to some historians the region where Islam first entered both the archipelago and Southeast Asia. Up until the late 19th century, the province was a fiercely independent sultanate that had existed as a sovereign entity for roughly 500 years. It was conquered by the Dutch only after a protracted war (1873–1903) that cost the lives of some 10,000 colonial troops. Following its emancipation from Dutch rule in 1949, the newly independent and Java-based Indonesian government made a vigorous attempt to consolidate control over the province, regarding it as being integral to the goal of a national, post-colonial unity.

Acehnese resistance to Jakarta is deeply rooted for several reasons: (1) the strong ethnic and religious identity of the Acehnese; (2) a widespread perception that the Acehnese have not benefited from the province's natural wealth and that industrial development projects have been introduced merely to provide employment opportunities to outsiders, especially from Java; (3) resentment at the Jakarta government's social migration policies, which were seen as an attempt to impose Javanese social, cultural, and economic domination; (4) the legacy of bitterness left by the government's often heavy-handed counterinsurgency efforts, particularly during the period the province was designated an area of military operations

(1990–1998); and (5) a rejection of the secular orientation of the Indonesian state, which is perceived to be at odds with Aceh's strict Sunni form of Islamic observance.[1]

The GAM Insurgency

Acehnese disillusion with centralized rule was first expressed in support for the wider Darul Islam rebellion in the 1950s. Acehnese demands were partially met by Indonesia's acceptance of "special region" status for the province in 1959, which endorsed a degree of official respect for local Islamic law and custom. Nonetheless, ongoing dissatisfaction with the secular and centralizing orientation of the Jakarta regime was exploited by a group of hard-line separatists, organized under the name of the Gerakan Aceh Merdeka, or Free Aceh Movement, to initiate a rebellion in the mid-1970s. The GAM insurgency waxed and waned throughout the Suharto era, but failed to develop a significant popular base. There was a spike in the violence at the end of the decade of the 1980s with the infiltration into the province of scores of Libyan-trained Acehnese. In 1990, the Suharto government declared Aceh a theater of military operations and mounted a large-scale counterinsurgency campaign that largely destroyed the GAM guerrillas, but at the cost of more than a thousand civilian casualties (Human Rights Watch, 2001b, p. 8).[2]

The fall of Suharto gave the insurgency a new lease on life. With the lifting of many of the New Order's political controls and the new freedom of expression, assembly, and association, not only the GAM, but also pro-independence political and student organizations and human rights NGOs were able to mobilize popular support and established links among themselves. The GAM exploited the disarray in Jakarta and the growth of popular support for independence in Aceh to expand its presence in the province, step up its attacks, and begin to set up an alternative administration. The most recent Indonesian intelligence sources put the GAM's current armed strength at about

---

[1] In the case of Aceh, as in the Muslim insurgencies in the Philippines and Thailand, a strong religious identity coincides with ethnic, political, and socioeconomic status. The analytical challenge in these cases is to determine the extent to which religion is fundamental in explaining the outbreak of the insurgencies.

[2] The numbers given for the GAM infiltrators range from 80 to more than 100.

1,000 to 1,200 fighters with weapons.[3] A knowledgeable NGO source, who is well acquainted with developments in Aceh, has estimated that a reasonable figure is 2,000 to 3,000 fighters scattered throughout Aceh with modern firearms readily available for about half the fighters at any one time. In addition, according to the same source, the GAM can count on sanctuary and logistical support from many village Acehnese.

The GAM is not a unified organization. Some of its elements are dedicated to the independence of Aceh. Others may be seeking a loosening of Jakarta's grip on the province. Among these elements are student and civil society sectors that see the GAM as a force fighting for a less intrusive central government. Other elements are little more than criminal gangs taking advantage of the GAM as a cover for their operations.

Both the GAM and the security forces employ violence against civilians to coerce support for their own side or deter support for the other side. GAM violence, however, is more targeted, reflecting better intelligence on local people and conditions. The security forces, especially the paramilitary police units (Brimob), appear to be much more indiscriminate in their use of the violence, frequently resorting to collective punishments in retaliation for attacks on their members. Since such indiscriminate actions further alienate the local population, the GAM will sometimes target security personnel precisely to incite violence by government troops against civilians. Both sides have command and control problems, but the discipline problems of the security forces seem to be greater than are those of the GAM. The GAM by and large appears to more willing to punish members who are found guilty of crimes against civilians. The army is trying to improve the behavior of its troops, giving better training to the troops sent to the field, including human rights training and more careful printed guidance on rules of engagement. There is a greater incidence of discipline problems with the Brimob, which is neither as well trained nor as disciplined as the military and, at the same time, receives the brunt of the GAM attacks.

---

[3]According to confidential Indonesian intelligence sources, February 2002.

By the middle of 2001, when the last extension of the "humanitarian pause" (discussed in the next section) expired, the GAM had developed a strong presence in six of Aceh's most populous and wealthiest districts (Human Rights Watch, 2001b, p. 7). GAM guerrillas also attacked strategic economic targets, particularly the important Exxon-Mobil natural gas facilities near Lhokseumawe in northern Aceh. Gunmen have hijacked the company's trucks and vans traveling among company sites in northern Aceh 50 times since 1999. In September 2000, the rebels began to target company buses carrying employees from the town to the gas fields. At first, the buses were stopped and burned. When Indonesian soldiers began to escort the buses, the separatists attacked them and detonated roadside pipe bombs. In March 2001, ExxonMobil closed down the three offshore fields, and evacuated employees not native to the area. Production did not resume until July, after 2,500 Indonesian troops were deployed to protect the facilities. The cost to Indonesia in lost revenues was on the order of $100 million a month ("ExxonMobil, in Fear …," 2001).[4]

Jakarta's Response

The Habibie and Wahid governments attempted to conciliate the Acehnese through dialogue and political concessions short of granting the province independence. The Habibie government lifted the province's status as a theater of military operations and ordered the withdrawal of forces not directly assigned to the territorial com-

---

[4]Operating in an area of armed conflict raises difficult issues for ExxonMobil and other companies in a similar situation. The company, indirectly through the Indonesian state oil company Pertamina, pays the soldiers that guard it and provides them with vehicles and other equipment; this renders ExxonMobil vulnerable to accusations of complicity in human rights abuses when they occur. (ExxonMobil was in fact sued by a Washington, D.C.–based human rights organization under the Alien Tort Claims Act for complicity in human rights violations committed by the security forces protecting its installations. The company strongly denied the allegations. Under the arrangement with Pertamina, Pertamina is solely responsible for security ["ExxonMobil Rides Out Squalls …," 2001].) As with other companies in a similar situation, ExxonMobil has tried to maintain neutrality in the conflict, but almost any action it takes is bound to be viewed by one side as favoring the other. The production shutdown in 2001, for instance, created friction with the Indonesian government, which suspected that the company was using the shutdown to extract better business terms.

mands in Aceh.[5] Habibie himself traveled to Aceh in March 1999 to apologize for past abuses and appointed an independent commission, composed largely of Acehnese, to investigate the violence in the province.[6] Law 22 of 1999 on Regional Autonomy, passed under Habibie and implemented during the Wahid administration, restored Aceh's Special Autonomous Region status—a broad grant of autonomy that included the application of Islamic law (*sharia*) to the Muslim inhabitants and compensation for past abuses by the security forces.[7]

Wahid broached the possibility of a referendum on the status of Aceh, but retreated after the idea came under heavy criticism by nationalists who feared another East Timor. Nevertheless, his government entered into negotiations with the GAM under the auspices of a Geneva-based conflict-resolution organization and signed a temporary cease-fire (officially called a "humanitarian pause") on May 15, 2000, subsequently extended through the first part of 2001.[8] The humanitarian pause, however, did not have a lasting effect in reducing the level of violence. The military believed that the GAM was taking advantage of the pause to expand its presence in the countryside and pressed for renewed military operations ("Army Wants to Crush ...," 2000).[9] In December 2000, Wahid visited Aceh in a last-ditch effort to

---

[5]Until January 2002, Aceh was part of Kodam I, which covered northern Sumatra, with headquarters in Medan. The province has two Korems, one in Bandar Aceh and one in Lhokseumawe.

[6]Human Rights Watch points out that the members were appointed without consultation with victims' or human rights organizations and that the commission head was an Acehnese woman known to have business dealings with General Wiranto (Human Rights Watch, 2001b, p. 7). Nevertheless, the establishment of the commission represented a qualitative change in the Indonesian government's willingness to investigate and expose abuses. As the Human Rights Watch report notes, the commission published a detailed 500-page listing of thousands of cases of violence.

[7]From a presentation by Andi Mallarangeng, Council for Security Cooperation in the Asia Pacific (CSCAP) International Seminar on Indonesia's Future Challenges and Implications for the Region, Jakarta, March 8, 2000.

[8]The two sides agreed to cooperate in allowing NGOs to deliver humanitarian assistance to the Acehnese people.

[9]According to a confidential NGO source, the military had a point. After the humanitarian pause was signed, the GAM began to kidnap government officials, including even members of the provincial parliament, and "reeducated" the officials before returning them to their families. They stepped up raids on villages, murdered pro-government village leaders and, in the areas it controlled, required students (youths in

address Acehnese concerns and discontent, but failed to bridge the gap between disaffected Acehnese and the central government.

With no discernable progress in the peace talks with the GAM and in the face of strong public and military support for a firm government stance toward the Aceh rebels,[10] Wahid issued the Presidential Instruction Number 4 of April 11, 2001, which outlined a "comprehensive approach" to the security problem in Aceh. As the result, the structure of the security forces in Aceh was reorganized, with the national police and the army commander in Aceh given equal responsibility for operations, which were to be conducted by the police, but with full army support. From a baseline of 5,000 to 6,000 regular police and 4,000 to 5,000 territorial troops, mostly holding fixed positions, in the humanitarian pause period, the government deployed an additional 2,000 to 3,000 Brimob personnel and 11,000 to 12,000 nonorganic TNI troops at the end of 2000 and beginning of 2001. By April 2001, the government had deployed some 25,000 troops to the region, with Kostrad units engaged in field operations and Kopassus units providing intelligence support.

Intensified operations have led to an escalation of violence since mid-2001, which included stepped-up attacks and massacres of Javanese migrants by the GAM and executions of suspected GAM sympathizers and collective punishments by the TNI and pro-Indonesian militias in retaliation for the GAM attacks (Human Rights Watch, 2001b, p. 11). The intensity of the conflict could be measured by the number of casualties. According to an NGO source, from the fall of Suharto to the signing of the humanitarian pause in May 2000, the number of casualties rose and leveled at about 300 deaths and 600 wounded a year on each side. In 2001, the number of casualties began climbing again, for a total of 2,000 to 2,500 Acehnese fatalities in 2001.

The replacement of the conciliatory Wahid with the more nationalistic Megawati Sukarnoputri in July 2001 did not bring an immediate

---

the pesantren) to take four to six weeks of basic military training (i.e., indoctrination). A number of these youths were recruited into the GAM, which, according to the NGO source, probably doubled its strength during the humanitarian pause period.

[10]According to a Media Indonesia poll at the end of 2000, 74.26 percent of the respondents favored a firm position toward the GAM ("Army Wants to Crush ...," 2000).

hardening of the Jakarta government's policy toward Aceh. Despite her nationalistic credentials, Megawati demonstrated that she was prepared to take a pragmatic stance. She apologized to the people of Aceh and Papua for the excesses of the past and signed a law granting wide-ranging autonomy to the province (Law No. 18 of 2001).[11] The legislation grants Aceh a much higher portion of the proceeds from the provinces' resources. But just as Wahid's earlier efforts to conciliate the Acehnese had met with little success, Megawati's gestures toward the province did not fare any better. The GAM continued to insist that it would accept nothing short of independence and, at the beginning of 2002, the Megawati government turned toward a "security approach" to the insurgency problem.

The government's military campaign, at least initially, appears to have met with a degree of success. By the beginning of 2002, the TNI had succeeded in breaking up the GAM units into isolated bands and in gradually pushing them off the north coast highway (the axis of communications in the province), through central Aceh, and into the hills of Pidie district. On January 23, 2002, the GAM suffered a major blow when its longtime military commander, Abdullah Syafi'ie (also known as Teungku Lah) was killed in a gun battle with the security forces.[12] The GAM is now operating in smaller bands, primarily in the south and west coasts of Aceh, although there are reports that some of these bands may be reappearing in the north. All of the sources agree that these bands are not under unified central control; most are said to hold a common commitment to Acehnese independence, but some appear to have degenerated into criminals.[13]

---

[11] There is some controversy about the extent of the central government's concessions on autonomy. According to a source familiar with Acehnese perspectives, some of the draft autonomy laws that were considered were quite satisfactory to the Acehnese, but the law ultimately approved by the parliament fell short of expectations.

[12] Syafi'ie was the second GAM military commander. He joined GAM in 1976 and succeeded its first military commander, Chik Omar, when Omar himself was killed in 1982. Syafi'ie was replaced by a Libyan-trained commander, Muzakir Manaf. Manaf is described by an intelligence source as the brains behind Syafi'ie, but he lacks Syafi'ie's charisma and name recognition.

[13] Independent observers have reported cases of extortion and human rights violations by GAM units. Perhaps in recognition of this problem, the new GAM military commander, Muzakir Manaf, called for the "strengthening of our moral and military discipline" in his first public statement ("Swedish-Based GAM: ...," 2002).

In January 2002, the government reestablished the Aceh military command (Kodam), named Iskandar Muda after a 17th century Acehnese sultan, with headquarters in Banda Aceh. The Kodam had been closed in the mid-1980s as part of a countrywide reorganization and consolidation of territorial commands. An Acehnese officer, Brigadier General Djali Yusuf, was designated as Kodam commander. Human rights advocates criticized the reestablishment of the Kodam, fearing that it represented a return to the special-area-of-operations regime of the Suharto era.[14] But, in fact, the reestablishment of a Kodam in Aceh has symbolic rather than practical importance. It raises Aceh's profile in the Indonesian military structure and underscores Indonesia's determination to hold onto the province.[15] Nevertheless, as of this writing, the insurgency in Aceh is far from beaten down. According to a statement by the army's deputy chief of staff in March 2002, fighting was intensifying in four districts—North Aceh, Bireun, Pidie, and West Aceh ("1,850 Troops ...," 2002).

SEPARATISM IN PAPUA

Papua, which was known officially as Irian Jaya until January 1, 2002, is a sparsely populated but economically important component of Indonesia. It is the site of the world's largest gold and copper mining operation, and it has large gas and oil deposits. The province was not part of the original Indonesian state and had little in common with the rest of Indonesia. The majority of the two million inhabitants are Melanesians living in pre-modern conditions and speaking hundreds of separate languages and dialects.[16]

When Indonesia became independent in 1949, the Dutch insisted on retaining the province, then known as Netherlands New Guinea. The Dutch promoted a Papuan national identity, with a view to granting independence to the colony by 1970. But after a decade of agitation

---

[14]See McCulloch, 2002.

[15]In discussions with senior security officials in Jakarta in February 2002, the officials also cited "geopolitical factors" (i.e., the importance of guarding Indonesia's western approaches) for the reestablishment of the Aceh Kodam.

[16]It is fair to add that Indonesian nationalists regard Papua to be as much a part of Indonesia as any other province.

by Indonesian nationalists, armed infiltration, and the threat of the use of force, the province was annexed by Indonesia in a United Nations–sponsored process that many Papuans did not consider legitimate. In the 1969 "Act of Free Choice," 1,026 electors largely selected by the Indonesian authorities decided without a formal vote to confirm integration with Indonesia.[17]

Disaffection with Jakarta's rule, including domination of the provincial administration by outsiders, disregard for the local cultures, and exploitation of the province's vast natural resources under terms that did not benefit the local population created the conditions for a low-intensity insurgency led by the tribal-based Free Papua Organization (Organisasi Papua Merdeka or OPM). The OPM reportedly has a core of about 200 fighters in bands that are dispersed throughout the different areas in the immense province, mostly along the border with Papua New Guinea. They are not considered a threat to Jakarta's control, although their presence keeps alive the idea of Papuan independence and probably helps to stimulate the growing separatist sentiment among the native population.

As in the case of Aceh, the Suharto government pursued a "security approach" to the insurgency. There were major Indonesian military operations in the Jayawijaya highlands in 1977 to 1978, and in the Bela, Alama, Jila, and Mapenduma districts from 1996 to 1998. The use of the term "Papua" was forbidden, as were many forms of Papuan cultural expression (Human Rights Watch, 2001a, pp. 8–9).

The post-Suharto governments of presidents Habibie and Wahid followed an inconsistent approach of conciliation and repression. The Habibie government initially endorsed a "national dialogue" on Papua but suspended it when the province's leaders demanded independence at a meeting with the president in Jakarta. The Wahid government agreed to change the province's name from Irian Jaya, the name it was given after the Indonesian annexation, to Papua, but the MPR rejected the change at its August 2000 session. The name was finally bestowed officially with the start of regional autonomy on January 1, 2002. Wahid also agreed to let the Papuan flag, the Morning Star, be flown as long as it was flown below the Indonesian

---

[17]See Rabasa and Chalk (2001, p. 38). The most detailed recent analysis of political conditions in Irian Jaya is by the International Crisis Group (2001c).

flag. Wahid also apologized for past human rights abuses and replaced hard-line military and police commanders but, as in Aceh, he ruled out any prospect of independence (Human Rights Watch, 2001a, p. 40).

Wahid also provided state funds for a provincial assembly called the Great Consultation (Musyawarah Besar, or Mubes for short), which brought together about 400 regional representatives in February 2000 to discuss common concerns. As a result of the Mubes meeting, the Papuan Council Presidium was established to lead the independence movement. The presidium organized the Papuan Congress, an even larger gathering, involving some 500 official delegates and thousands of supporters from every part of the province as well as from exiled communities in Papua New Guinea, the Pacific islands, and Europe. The delegates adopted a resolution stating that the province's incorporation into Indonesia was illegal, and therefore null and void, and that West Papua—the delegates' name for the province—had been an independent state since 1961 (Human Rights Watch, 2001a, p. 10–11).

The leadership of the independence movement exemplified the transformation of the provincial political elites in the post-Suharto period. The leading personality in the movement and head of the Papuan Congress was Theys Eluay, a traditional chief who had served as a Golkar member of the provincial parliament and had voted for incorporation into Indonesia in the 1969 Act of Free Choice. As late as 1996, Theys was quoted as calling the idea of an independent Papuan state "rubbish." Theys was associated with the Satgas Papua militia, which was headed by one of his sons and believed to be funded by one of his associates in the Papuan Council Presidium, Yorrys Raweyai, a man of ethnic Chinese and Papuan background, who was deputy leader of the New Order youth organization, Pemuda Pancasila (International Crisis Group, 2002c, p. 12). Theys was killed under mysterious circumstances in November 2001 after he had reportedly attended a Heroes Day celebration with a Kopassus unit stationed in Jayapura.[18]

---

[18]According to Indonesian press reports, the Irian Jaya police revealed that military personnel had been involved in the murder, but the police could not investigate it because they lacked jurisdiction. In February 2002, the central government appointed an independent commission to probe into the murder. In its report to Coordinating

With the strengthening of pro-independence sentiment in the province, Jakarta shifted to a harder line toward separatists. In September 2000, the raising of the Morning Star flag was banned, but local authorities reportedly agreed to suspend the forcible removal of the flag until Papuan Council Presidium representatives had a chance to discuss the issue directly with Wahid. In October, security forces clashed with independent supporters when the authorities attempted to lower the Papuan flag at a number of Satgas Papua (pro-independence militia) posts in the Wamena area in the central highlands, a center of separatist sentiment. Thirty-two people were killed in the clashes and in an ensuing retaliatory attack by a Papuan crowd on a migrant neighborhood. The violence precipitated an exodus of settlers and coastal Papuans from Wamena (Human Rights Watch, 2001a, pp. 12–13; International Crisis Group, 2001c, pp. 7–8).[19] The government subsequently arrested more than 50 activists, including several leading members of the Papua Presidium, and announced it would not tolerate the raising of separatists flags or other acts indicating support for independence ("Jakarta Arrests ...," 2000). Simultaneous with the crackdown, the Jakarta government promoted an initiative to grant Special Autonomy for the province—an approach similar to that taken in Aceh—which was finally implemented on January 2, 2002.

Whether Jakarta's alternation of concessions and suppression will succeed in continuing to keep Papua a part of Indonesia will depend on whether the central government can deliver on autonomy and

---

Minister for Political and Security Affairs Yudhoyono on its preliminary findings, however, the commission said that it had not found any information on the involvement of Kopassus members in the murder ("KPN Reports Findings ...," 2002). On the other hand, reports published in *Tempo* link Theys' murder to competition among logging interests in the province. According to *Tempo*'s sources, the order for the execution was issued to a Kopassus team outside of the chain of command at the behest of a logging concessionaire with strong links to Kopassus and whose business interests were being obstructed by Theys ("Invisible Commander ...," and "Squeezed by ...," *Tempo*, April 2–8, 2002).

[19]As the result of the government-sponsored transmigration policy and the spontaneous migration from other parts of Indonesia, the non-Papuan population in Irian Jaya increased from 4 percent of the total population in 1971 to more than 20 percent in 1990, and may be as high as 40 percent today (Human Rights Watch, 2001a, p. 14). According to an estimate by a University of Cenderawasih (Jayapura) demographer cited in an ICG study, the settler communities constitute 30 percent of the population (International Crisis Group, 2001c, p. 6).

resource-sharing commitments in the Special Autonomy Law that entered into force on January 1, 2002, and whether the central authority will continue to weaken as the result of stresses on the Indonesian body politic. The situation may have evolved to the point, however, that concessions short of independence may not satisfy the pro-independence sectors, which now appear to include many of the tribal chiefs and the provincial elite.[20]

---

[20]According to a leaked Indonesian intelligence document cited in an ICG study, the Irian Jaya provincial government, including the former governor, who is the current Indonesian Ambassador to Mexico, had been contaminated by independence senti-ment (International Crisis Group, 2001c, p. 10).

PART III: THE FUTURE OF U.S.–INDONESIAN MILITARY RELATIONS

Chapter Eleven

THE ROCKY COURSE OF U.S.–INDONESIAN MILITARY RELATIONS

In Sukarno's latter years, Jakarta's policy of *konfrontasi* (confrontation) with Malaysia and growing alignment with the Soviet Union and the Beijing-line PKI generated a serious threat to U.S. security interests in the Asia-Pacific region. The fall of Sukarno and the emergence of Suharto's New Order marked a sharp change in the direction of Indonesia's foreign and security policy and in U.S.–Indonesian relations. Under Suharto, Indonesia became a pillar of the Association of Southeast Asian Nations, established in 1967, and of the new U.S.–backed informal regional security system. Despite the coincidence of U.S. and Indonesian strategic interests, the U.S.–Indonesian military relationship was subject to a number of shocks as the result of U.S. concerns—particularly in the Congress—over human rights issue and the Indonesian annexation of East Timor in 1974.

In 1992, the U.S. Congress cancelled $2.3 million in International Military Education and Training (IMET) funds for Indonesia, over the objections of the state and defense departments, as an expression of disapproval over the shooting of dozens of unarmed civilians at the Santa Cruz cemetery in Dili, East Timor, in November 1991. A program known as Expanded IMET (E-IMET), limited to training in judicial and human rights and other unobjectionable subjects, was restored in 1993. Ironically, the "Dili incident" laid the basis for the first instance in Indonesia in which the concept of command responsibility was applied to a field commander. In the aftermath of that tragic incident, an Army Military Honor Council held five officers responsible for the misconduct of soldiers under their command.[1]

Congress authorized E-IMET funding for Indonesia for fiscal years (FY) 1996 and 1997. However, Indonesia withdrew from the program in June 1997 over what President Suharto called "totally unfair criticism" of Indonesian human rights practices by the U.S. Congress and to eliminate what Suharto perceived as a contentious political issue marring the more important and broader issues of the country-to-country relationship.

After 1993, the United States continued to provide training to Indonesian military units under the Joint Combined Exchange and Training (JCET) program, which did not fall within the categories of prohibited activities. Those "soldier-to-soldier" activities continued on a reduced basis under the aegis of the U.S. Pacific Command until 1998, when the JCET program with Indonesia was suspended after it came under political attack in the United States. With few exceptions (some Indonesian officers continued to be trained in the United States at Indonesian expense), Indonesian military personnel have had little exposure to U.S. training since then.[2]

During the Clinton administration, internal U.S. government reviews proposed the restoration of full IMET for Indonesia, but divisions within the administration and congressional opposition blocked action. U.S. military equipment sales were similarly constrained by human rights controversies. In 1994, the United States banned the sale of small and light arms and riot-control equipment to Indonesia. The ban was the first across-the-board prohibition on any type of weapons sale to Indonesia. In 1995 and 1996, the list of prohibited

---

[1]The most senior of the five officers was Major General Sintong Panjaitan, the Kodam commander responsible for operations in eastern Indonesia. A national hero as a result of his commanding the special forces operation to free a hijacked Garuda Airlines aircraft in Bangkok, many felt he was made a scapegoat to satisfy international critics. The other officers who were punished were the task force commander in East Timor (a brigadier general), the task force intelligence officer, the battalion commander of the troops involved, and the military district commander (all lieutenant colonels). The two platoon leaders of the troops who did the shooting at the Santa Cruz cemetery were convicted by court-martial of failing to control their soldiers and given light prison sentences. Eight soldiers and policemen were also convicted.

[2]Lieutenant General Agus Widjojo, presently vice chairman of the MPR, was one of the last Indonesian officers to attend the U.S. National Defense University.

items was expanded to include helicopter-mounted equipment and armored personnel carriers. Congressional notification of the sale of nine F-16 aircraft (originally built for Pakistan) was repeatedly postponed until in 1997 the Suharto government cancelled the F-16 purchase. Indonesia subsequently announced plans for the acquisition of 12 Russian SU-30MK and 8 Mi-17 helicopters, but suspended those plans after the onset of the 1997–1998 Asian economic crisis.

In the wake of the violence in East Timor after the August 1999 independence referendum, the Clinton administration suspended the transfer of defense articles and services to Indonesia as well as military exercises and exchanges. Section 589 of the Fiscal Year 2000 Foreign Operations appropriations (extended and expanded in the FY2001 and FY2002 legislation, and commonly known as the Leahy amendment after its author Senator Patrick Leahy, [D-Vermont]) put into law the ban on military training and weapons transfers. The Leahy Amendment requires the U.S. president to certify to Congress that Indonesia has made progress in addressing specific actions related to human rights before IMET funding and government-to-government military sales can be resumed.

Specifically, the requirements of the legislation are that Indonesia end support for pro-Indonesia militia groups in West Timor; that such militia groups be prevented from making incursions into East Timor and from terrorizing refugee camps in West Timor; that Indonesia repatriate refugees wishing to return to East Timor; and that Indonesian military personnel and militia members responsible for specific acts of violence in East Timor be identified and punished. In 2001, Congress extended these conditions and added three more requirements, including transparency in the Indonesian military budget. (See the appendix for an analysis of the likelihood that Indonesia will be able to meet the conditions of the Leahy Amendment).

Following Under Secretary of State Thomas R. Pickering's visit to Jakarta in March 2000, the Clinton administration began to take some steps to resume military cooperation, within the scope allowed by legislative prohibitions. There was a limited resumption of Indonesian participation in combined exercises—some ten Indonesian air force officers participated in the annual Cobra Gold exercise in Thailand (a large, annual multilateral exercise involving the United States, Thailand, and Singapore). In September 2000, the United

States granted a waiver for commercial sales of C-130 spare parts. The administration also approved the sale of spare parts for CN-235 aircraft being assembled in Indonesia for sale to South Korea. However, this limited progress in engagement with the Indonesian military was set back again when three United Nations workers in West Timor were killed by militia in September 2000.

U.S.–INDONESIAN MILITARY RELATIONS IN THE ERA OF TERRORISM

The landscape of U.S.–Indonesian military relations was transformed by the September 11 terrorist attacks and the subsequent global war on terrorism. The Leahy Amendment and related policy restrictions on military engagement with Indonesia remain in place, but the context of the U.S.–Indonesian relationship and U.S. policy priorities regarding Indonesia shifted in consonance with the shift in the United States' global priorities. President Megawati was the first leader of a major Muslim country to visit Washington after September 11. The invitation to Megawati to visit Washington, less than two months after succeeding President Wahid, reflected the Bush administration's increased attention to Indonesia and was meant to highlight the United States' support for the new Indonesian government and Indonesian democracy.

Megawati's visit also took place in the context of another review of U.S. policy toward Indonesia, which concluded with a decision to deepen engagement and move to restore some ties with the Indonesian military. In the joint communiqué issued by President George W. Bush and President Megawati during her visit, the two presidents recognized the Indonesian military's important role as a national institution and the importance of military reform in Indonesia's democratic transition. They agreed to expand contacts and resume regular meetings between the U.S. and Indonesian militaries to support Indonesia's efforts at reform and professionalization of the military. President Bush expressed his commitment to work with Congress to allocate $400,000 in E-IMET for Indonesia. President Megawati, in turn, expressed full appreciation that Indonesia must resolve outstanding issues relating to past human rights violations, especially in conflict zones (The White House, 2001).

Jakarta approved overflights of Indonesian air space by U.S. aircraft supporting the operations in Afghanistan and increased security for U.S. personnel and facilities in Indonesia. Megawati, however, retreated from high-profile support of the U.S.-led global war on terrorism after the United States began military operations against terrorist targets in Afghanistan and Muslim political parties and organizations opposed the U.S. actions. Her own vice president, Hamzah Haz, leader of the Muslim-oriented PPP, departed from her position by calling on the United States to stop its military campaign ("Hamzah Demands ...," 2001).

The Megawati government's reluctance to aggressively investigate individuals and groups associated with Al Qaeda generated some frustration in Washington. Nevertheless, the United States would like to work more closely with the Indonesian armed forces in the counterterrorism war by using a significant part of a $21 million program sponsored by Senator Daniel K. Inouye (D-Hawaii) for training regional forces in counterterrorism operations in the newly established Regional Defense Counterterrorism Fellowship Program.[3] The U.S. military can provide training in tactics, intelligence gathering and analysis, and international cooperation. The TNI can provide its own well-trained forces, who will be expected to take the lead in any military operations against terrorist cells that may be found in Indonesia.

The Inouye legislation appears to directly conflict with the restrictions of the Leahy Amendment insofar as the counterterrorist training program pertains to cooperative training with the TNI. Fortunately, there are some circumstances that should allow U.S. interests in counterterrorism to meld with continued U.S. principles on human rights considerations and TNI accountability:

- First, there is a possibility that the long-delayed ad hoc tribunal, which convened in February 2002, will in fact convict a number of accused officers, possibly including some (if not all) general

---

[3]Statement of Admiral Dennis C. Blair, U.S. Navy, Commander in Chief, U.S. Pacific Command, before the House International Relations Committee Subcommittee on East Asia and the Pacific and Subcommittee on Middle East and South Asia on U.S. Pacific Command Posture, Washington, D.C., February 27, 2002.

officers on the list of suspects.[4] Indonesia does not want to risk further offending the United Nations, which is on record that it could convene an international tribunal on East Timor abuses if Indonesia fails to act. Some senior TNI officers also understand the damage to Indonesia's reputation if it fails to address the accountability issue. The alleged offenses are violations of the TNI's own regulations and procedures, which could make it easier to secure convictions without the appearance of giving in to foreign pressure. However, the fact that the TNI has allowed its military readiness to be damaged before it would offer up senior officers in human rights trials shows the limitations of a sanctions policy in producing the desired outcomes.

- Second, many of the restrictions on military cooperation with Indonesia are based on policy rather than legislation. There is considerable scope for assistance that the U.S. government—including the Department of Defense—could provide to the Indonesian intelligence community outside of the Leahy Amendment restriction.

MEASURING THE EFFECTS OF ENGAGEMENT

The effects of engagement, which are reflected in personal relationships, trust, and access, are hard to measure but are nonetheless real, as has been demonstrated in the ability of the U.S. military to influence counterparts in political crisis in Thailand and the Philippines over the past two decades. The close personal and institutional ties that characterize the U.S. relationship with the Thai and Philippine militaries are lacking in Indonesia as the result of a "lost decade" in which there was little U.S. training of Indonesian military personnel.

A discussion of the effects of engagement—particularly through IMET—can be structured in terms of influence, access, and professionalization, three topics we cover next.

---

[4]An NGO source familiar with the process acknowledged privately that there is no hard evidence linking former armed forces commander General Wiranto to the violence in East Timor. Recent leaks of sensitive intelligence information in Australia have implicated a number of senior officers not formally accused by the Indonesian authorities.

Influence

Most military professionals and analysts with experience in military-to-military relations believe that the IMET program is an important tool for the United States in influencing the outlook and attitudes of foreign military personnel. The absence of Indonesian officers from U.S. military schools at all levels for the past ten years has meant that virtually none of the candidates for senior TNI posts in the coming years have been trained in the United States and, therefore, are unfamiliar with the U.S. political, social, and military environments. Senior U.S.–trained Indonesian officers themselves lament the fact that their successors do not have firsthand knowledge of the United States and its concerns and interests.

Foreign military officers who attend U.S. military schools under the IMET program train to American standards alongside American military personnel. A high level of understanding of the English language is required for this training. Participants in the program are exposed to the American professional military establishment and American values, including respect for internationally established norms in human rights, civilian control of the armed forces, and the rule of law.[5]

How exposure to American values and American practices translates into influence is, of course, a complicated and controversial issue. Like all civilian international visitor programs, the case for IMET rests on the premise that the experience would produce intangible benefits, in this case by educating the foreign student about the role of the military in American society. Working and studying beside American military officers for months at a time, in this view, provides subtle but ingrained exposure to the American model of civil-military relations. Without this exposure, there will likely be fewer voices to balance extreme nationalists and xenophobic elements within the TNI.

---

[5]This discussion on the IMET program is partially based on Haseman (1998).

Access

The role of IMET in facilitating U.S. access to Indonesian military leaders is less open to question. The enhanced person-to-person relationships between American officers and their foreign classmates have repeatedly been cited as being of great value in future years when those young officers have risen to the highest levels of their respective armed forces and national government establishments. In Indonesia, the capability to gain the ear of senior TNI officers as the result of shared experiences and friendship provides a more meaningful opportunity to discuss—and perhaps influence—issues of importance to both countries. While it is naive to assume that personal relationships alone sway TNI decisionmaking, such relationships are an important factor in Indonesian culture and at a minimum improve the prospects of receiving a receptive hearing by Indonesian military leaders.

Professionalization

On a purely professional level, foreign students are trained in military management and military skills. This exposure to U.S. military professionalism helps to build a common understanding of military terminology, weapons systems, and management expertise, critical to military interoperability with friends and allies around the world.

Chapter Twelve

STRATEGIC SCENARIOS FOR INDONESIA AND THEIR IMPLICATIONS

Although Indonesia's future is highly uncertain, several conditions can be expected to hold for the next several years:

- First, a sustained economic recovery is not on the horizon. Although the economy (i.e., the GDP) grew at a rate of 3.5 percent in 2001, the underlying causes of the country's economic weakness—large private and public debt and the insolvency of much of the corporate and banking sectors—remain unresolved.

- Second, the political system will remain under stress. The Megawati government has been unable to make headway on economic reform or to show much administrative competency, but the opposition parties have yet to develop any coherent strategies for governing the country. The decentralization process, if not properly managed, has the potential to be greatly destabilizing.

- Third, the issue of the role of Islam in politics—which, as already noted in this report, goes back to the fundamental question of the nature of the Indonesian state—will continue to be a divisive issue and could have significant impact on the 2004 and subsequent elections. Will Megawati, if she is reelected, continue to be dependent on the Muslim political parties for her parliamentary majority? If the Golkar organization (the political instrument of the New Order, which has been trying to recreate itself as a viable post-Suharto party) collapses, will Islam form the basis for a new political bloc?

- Fourth, the military will continue to play a key role in keeping the political process on track, and may be forced into a more overt political role if the country's political and institutional framework weakens further.

In the following sections, we postulate five strategic scenarios for Indonesia, each of which has important consequences for the Indonesian military and for U.S.–Indonesian relations.

SCENARIO 1: DEMOCRATIC CONSOLIDATION

In the best-case scenario, Indonesia continues to develop along a secular, democratic trajectory, makes progress in resolving some of the critical problems in the economy, and satisfies demands for provincial autonomy without losing central control of its macro-economic policy. In the area of civil-military relations, there is more-effective civilian control of the military through better oversight of military affairs by the minister of defense and the parliament. If economic growth resumed and the necessary resources became available, a greater proportion of the Indonesian military's expenditures could be funded from the state budget, rather than from off-budget sources. In the short term, it would be unrealistic to expect the military to withdraw from its economic activities, but there could be greater transparency in the operation of military businesses. There would also be some movement away from the territorial structure, beginning in areas where that structure is no longer needed, such as the island of Java.

Policy Implications for Counterterrorism

This scenario offers the best prospects for counterterrorism cooperation, a key post–September 11 U.S. priority. Indonesian cooperation against international terrorism need not involve the deployment of U.S. forces in a training or advisory role, as in the case of the Philippines, but it would involve Indonesia's taking meaningful action to prevent the country from being used as a sanctuary by members of international terrorist networks—the sort of actions, for instance, that the governments of Malaysia and Singapore have taken. A comprehensive attack on terrorism would also involve taking action against national groups such as the Laskar Jihad that, while not classified as international terrorist groups themselves, are linked in one way or another to terrorist networks.

Policy Implications for Engagement

With Indonesia actively participating in the war against terrorism in Southeast Asia and making headway in economic and military reform, the United States would be in a stronger position to move forward toward normal military relations with Indonesia and to bring Indonesia as a full partner into the evolving network of U.S.–led security arrangements in the Asia-Pacific regions. The Leahy amendment (see Chapter Eleven) may continue to constrain certain types of U.S. assistance to Indonesia. However, the amendment's focus on the 1999 East Timor violence and associated events is increasingly outdated, and there are good prospects that Indonesia may be able to meet the conditions of the Leahy Amendment or that the U.S. Congress will lift some or all of the restrictions. (See the appendix for a further discussion.)

The prospect of closer engagement with Indonesia raises some important issues:

- What assistance should be provided to the Indonesia military and security services for counterterrorism operations?

- What kind of intelligence information and what kind of equipment and training should be given?

- Would the United States be willing to provide assistance that could be directed against Acehnese rebels, for instance?

- How does the United States strike a balance between what the Indonesians want and what it believes the Indonesians need?

- What kinds of assistance should the United States provide to assist in military reform?

SCENARIO 2: MUDDLING THROUGH

This second scenario builds on trends that are already evident. Indonesia continues on a democratic path, but fails to make meaningful progress on economic, political, and military reform. The structural problems in the Indonesian economy are not addressed. Military reform comes to a halt after the initial impetus for reform, which had been generated by domestic and international public pressure after the fall of Suharto, slows down. The military is formally under civilian authority, but retains a decisive voice in national security decisionmaking.

In this scenario, the government is not successful in negotiating a political solution to the problem of separatism in Aceh and Papua and continues to resort to a "security approach." Jakarta has the military power to prevent the separatists from seriously threatening its control of these provinces, but is obliged to mount costly counterinsurgency campaigns that overextend the military's resources. The pressure on the military inevitably leads to overreaction and human rights violations which, in turn, generate criticism by human rights advocates and strain Jakarta's relationship with the United States and other Western countries.

This scenario reflects the current situation in Indonesia and is therefore the most relevant to current policymakers.

Policy Implications for Counterterrorism

Under the conditions in this scenario, a weak Indonesian government would continue to find it difficult to take meaningful action against terrorists and radical Islamic groups. The Jakarta government might well continue to straddle the fence, seeking to do the minimum required on the counterterrorism front to placate the United States and regional critics, but not enough to provoke a backlash from Muslims.

Policy Implications for Engagement

It might still be possible to argue that the overriding strategic objectives of promoting democracy and stability should be determining U.S. policy. But realistically, lack of progress in three critical areas—the economy, military reform, and counterterrorism—would make it difficult to overcome opposition to engagement with Indonesia from the U.S. Congress and others. Engagement would probably have to consist of a series of individual military activities limited to what the policy traffic would bear rather than a more ambitious effort to bring Indonesia into a strategic security framework.

This scenario raises the following questions, which are more difficult to address than the issues raised by Scenario 1:

- How do constraints on assistance to Indonesia affect counter-terrorism cooperation?

- What are the incentives for the Indonesians to cooperate on high-profile counterterrorism operations?

- As noted in Chapter Eleven, how should the Inouye legislation that addresses counterterrorism training be reconciled with the Leahy Amendment restrictions?

- What do the Indonesians need to do to be in compliance with the conditions of the Leahy Amendment?

- What options can the United States develop to prevent further deterioration of the U.S.–Indonesian relationship?

SCENARIO 3: RETURN TO AUTHORITARIAN RULE

The "muddling through" scenario presented in the previous section should be considered to be among the better-case scenarios. The fragile economy and a breakdown of order could generate more negative scenarios. One such negative scenario would be a return to authoritarian rule. There are some powerful factors that militate against this outcome, at least in the short term, including the backlash against Suharto's 32-year rule, the emergence of new political and civil society forces, and the discredit suffered by the military and the security services as a result of their association with the Suharto regime. Nevertheless, continued inability of the new democratic institutions to deliver stability, competent government, and economic growth could generate a demand for the return of a strong ruler.

Any return to authoritarian rule must have the backing of the military, but the military would prefer to stay in the background. Only a catastrophic political collapse would compel the military to assume effective control of the government. If that were to happen, the most likely model would be a military-technocratic government, with economic policymaking in the hands of nonpolitical technocrats and eventual return to formal civilian control.

A second negative scenario could be an alliance of the military with political sectors, such as one or more of the Islamic parties. That was the Pakistani model before September 11, when there was considerable infiltration of the Pakistani government and the military by militant Islamic forces. Some secular Indonesians are concerned that the "creeping Islamization" that the country is undergoing (see Scenario 4 later in this chapter) over time could make the Islamic parties an acceptable partner for the military or a military faction. This scenario could precipitate the secession from Indonesia of areas in which Christians are a majority or a substantial minority, or could result in civil war.

A third version of the scenario might be one that follows the "Burmese model." As the name of this scenario suggests, it would constitute a very repressive form of military rule in which the leaders try to isolate the country from Western influences. This government would try to bring the press, political parties, and independent sectors of society under its control and repress groups it considers subversive. This model of authoritarian government could come about if the military were convinced that its institutional integrity or the country's survival was at stake.

Policy Implications for Counterterrorism

An authoritarian government might be better able to take more forceful action against terrorist and radical networks than would a weak democratic government. Such a government could, for instance, implement more forceful internal security laws. On the other hand, this scenario would probably also bring into play legal or policy restrictions on the United States' interaction with Indonesia that would severely hamper meaningful cooperation on counterterrorism efforts.

Policy Implications for Engagement

The policy response by the United States and other Western democracies to this scenario would almost certainly be a call for a return to democratic rule. U.S. and other Western policymakers would want to develop a package of incentives and sanctions to bring about a rapid return to civilian rule, but they would be confronted with a dilemma. While the Indonesian military will have a decisive voice in determining the pace and timing of a return to democratic government, U.S. domestic and international pressures will drive the U.S. administration in the direction of sanctions and curtailment of ties with the TNI.

The U.S. administration's ability to engage the TNI would depend on the specific circumstances of the turn of events in Indonesia. A "benign" intervention by the military to restore order and security, possibly even with the acquiescence of the civilian authorities, would be far less disruptive to cooperative bilateral relations than an open overthrow of the established government or an intervention accompanied by large-scale violence and bloodshed. Similarly, a situation in which there are realistic prospects of restoring a democratic government would give more scope to a policy of engagement than one in which there is no pretense of a return to democratic rule.

SCENARIO 4: RADICAL ISLAMIC INFLUENCE OR CONTROL

A radical Islamic takeover is possible, but should be considered a low-probability scenario at this stage. It would be opposed by secularists in the political establishment and in the military and probably by most Indonesian Muslims themselves, the vast majority of whom are moderate and do not support the radicals' agenda. However, progressive Islamization—defined as increased influence of Islam in politics and more overt manifestations of religiosity in public behavior—would be entirely possible.

In the view of some close observers of the Indonesian political scene, it is only a matter of time before the pattern of political competition in Indonesia (with the Muslim political parties seeking to promote an Islamic agenda and the government and moderates unwilling to actively oppose them) opens more space for radical Islam, especially if the economic recession continues. Indonesian officials say that they are concerned about the emergence of radical and fundamentalist groups over the past few years and are working with moderate Muslim leaders to contain this trend. However, many moderate Indonesians express frustration that the government and moderate

Muslims have allowed the more militant sectors of the Muslim community to influence and, to some extent, set the political agenda.

Policy Implications for Counterterrorism

A Jakarta government under the influence or control of radical Islamic groups would have an anti-Western orientation. It would support or encourage Islamic fundamentalist political forces in Malaysia and Muslim separatists in the Philippines and southern Thailand. The resulting upsurge of political Islam in Southeast Asia would also result in the isolation of Singapore, with destabilizing consequences for the whole region.

Policy Implications for Engagement

It would not be realistic to expect any meaningful U.S. or Western engagement with the Indonesia military in this scenario, although the United States or some of Indonesia's neighbors may be able to develop back channels to officers in the Indonesian military who might oppose the Indonesian government's orientation.

The United States would be forced to develop more intelligence on hostile groups in Indonesia and the intentions and capabilities of those groups and to provide more intensive surveillance of the seas around Indonesia to interdict the movement of terrorists and arms. This effort could take the form of multilateral initiatives with regional friends and allies. In extremis, it might be necessary to conduct direct counterterrorist operations in Indonesia if intelligence determines that groups operating in Indonesia pose a threat to the United States, its citizens, or its allies.

SCENARIO 5: RADICAL DECENTRALIZATION

An exhausted or weakened central government under pressure from the outer regions might permit, or be forced to accept, more wide-ranging autonomy initiatives that replicate the Acehnese-Papuan special privileges across the archipelago. This scenario might evolve into a central state that controls, nominally, only defense, foreign affairs, fiscal policy, and the core legal system. Such an Indonesian state would be inherently unstable as centrifugal pressures, unchecked by coercive power, force it apart. The Yugoslav, Soviet, and Czechoslovak examples are the most current models of forces working from within to break apart multiethnic countries by using various degrees of violence. Countries such as Nigeria struggle with a complex challenge such as this for the same reasons that Indonesia does—these countries are artifacts of European colonial processes that have been seeking, even after they have gained their independence, to forge a national identity that transcends their disparate parts.

General Policy Implications

This scenario, in contrast to its more benign analog—a federation— would make it harder to achieve counterterrorism objectives because the central government might be powerless to control activities of terrorists or extremists in the provinces. The situation in some Indonesian provinces could become analogous to the situation in Pakistan's tribal areas on the Afghan border.

The consequences for engagement would be ambiguous and would depend on the role that the Indonesian military plays in a decentralized Indonesia. If the military is seen as the sole guarantor of order or as the force preventing Indonesia from falling apart (see the next section), the geopolitical case for engagement (or, at least, the consequences of failing to engage) would be difficult to ignore.

SCENARIO 6: DISINTEGRATION

Territorial disintegration could be the end stage of some of the downside scenarios described in the previous sections. Weak government and chaotic conditions would make the central government less relevant and reduce the incentives for wealthy provinces to acquiesce in a subordinate economic and political relationship with Jakarta. This is, in fact, what is happening now to some extent.

Disintegration could also come about as the result of a split or collapse in the military, which might fracture along one or more of the many divides in Indonesian society. Or disintegration could follow the outbreak of large-scale violence and secessionist or dissident revolts in the outer islands that the overextended Indonesian military would be unable to control.

General Policy Implications

Disintegration would have catastrophic consequences for counterterrorism efforts and regional stability. It would result in severe economic dislocation and an increase in illegal migration, piracy, and international crime. It would also significantly increase the likelihood of major humanitarian crises requiring a response by the international community.

Separatist and irredentist groups throughout the region would be encouraged to press their agendas and could find support in some of the new entities that emerge from the Indonesian shipwreck. ASEAN would be severely weakened or destroyed as an effective regional organization. Regional states would be forced to fall back on their own resources to provide for their security, increasing the likelihood of interstate conflict.

In the counterterrorism arena, the fragments of a failed Indonesian state could become havens for terrorists and troublemakers of all stripes, creating huge challenges for U.S. counterterrorism policy.

Chapter Thirteen

GOALS FOR INDONESIAN MILITARY REFORM AND ELEMENTS OF A U.S. ENGAGEMENT STRATEGY

The tensions that Indonesia is currently experiencing are certain to continue and, as noted in Chapter Twelve, could lead to a variety of outcomes. Given the importance of stability and orderly change in Indonesia, the United States and the U.S. military would do well to engage the Indonesian military in order to shape its response to changes in the country's political environment and to hedge against the downside of change.

Cooperation between the U.S. and Indonesian military has been intermittent and plagued by tensions over East Timor and human rights issues and by congressionally mandated sanctions. However, the democratization of Indonesia since the fall of Suharto has created opportunities for closer military interaction. This interaction offers a base upon which the Indonesian military can move forward with military reform and deal constructively with the challenge of rebuilding civil-military relations on democratic principles.

GOALS FOR INDONESIAN MILITARY REFORM

Among the goals the TNI sets for itself are internal reform, development of well-educated leaders who support democracy over dictatorships, and support for civilian institutions that will preserve national unity and internal security. The U.S. military's program of engagement should focus on providing the Indonesian military with the doctrines, training, and resources to implement its reform program and to develop the capability to defend the country's unity and territorial integrity.

Reform of the Territorial System

The TNI's leaders believe that it would be irresponsible to give up its political powers and influence until a suitable and effective successor institution is in place and can assume responsible governance. The much-criticized territorial system is a case in point. The position of TNI chief of staff for territorial affairs has been downgraded to an assistant post, and a public commitment has been made to turn over most of the territorial system functions to the police and civil government. However, both civilian and military leaders agree that civilian institutions are not yet ready to assume these functions.

The military leadership has conducted several public seminars at which the future of the territorial system was of primary interest. Both the military leadership and civilian critics agree that the lowest levels of the system—the village, subdistrict, and district levels—will eventually be disbanded. Among those expressing this view was Lieutenant General Agus Widjojo, who served for several years as the TNI chief of staff for territorial affairs ("Kaster TNI ...," 2001).

The goal for the TNI in this area should be to begin the process of dismantling the territorial structure in those areas where the security conditions do not require a continued military role.

Civil-Military Relations

Political changes are already underway throughout the TNI as an institution. Perhaps the most important of these changes is the formal renunciation of the controversial dwifungsi (dual function) doctrine under which the armed forces had an official, formal political mission. Dwifungsi was originally intended to provide much-needed political leadership to a country foundering in the economic and political quagmire of the Sukarno years. After gaining the presidency, however, Suharto used the dwifungsi concept—which by then had become military doctrine and enshrined in national law—to justify extending the military's tentacles into virtually every element of civil society. In so doing, the armed forces became the base of support for the regime, the enforcer of Suharto's will, and the political power behind the throne.

The actual effects of the elimination of dwifungsi from TNI doctrine must await the passage of time, but the TNI should be encouraged and helped to deal constructively with the challenge of building a new model of civil-military relations based on democratic principles. A great part of the burden of building this new model, however, lies with the civilian leadership. The civilian sector needs to develop the depth and range of knowledge in defense matters that would make its views respected by the soldiers. It is also incumbent upon the Indonesian government to ensure that civilians appointed to senior positions in the Indonesian Department of Defense have the requisite expertise.

Military Financing

As has been recognized in other countries such as Thailand and China, the military will not become fully professional until it withdraws from its various economic activities. In the case of Indonesian, given the country's budgetary difficulties, it is not realistic to expect that the TNI could be funded entirely out of the state budget in the near term. Therefore, while this should be a long-term goal, the most practical solution for the present would be to increase transparency and accountability in military-run enterprises. This would reduce opportunities for corruption, quantify the true costs of operating the military, allow for more rational planning, and lay the groundwork for the eventual phasing out of off-budget expenditures.

Human Rights

TNI reformers have also begun to reform military education by including human rights and rules of engagement in military training. But, as the International Crisis Group has noted, the military has not imposed penalties for the violation of these rules, particularly in conflict areas such as Aceh and Papua (International Crisis Group, 2001d). The more thoughtful TNI leaders recognize the importance of improving the military's human rights performance, both to defuse international criticism and to restore the link between the army and the people, a link that has always been at the heart of the

TNI doctrine. A problem lies in the TNI's corporate culture of loyalty up and down the chain of command and the cultural aversion to directly criticizing anyone, even subordinates, for fear of weakening loyalty and patronage ties.[1] Change in this area will be slow to evolve and would be most successfully promoted through the use of positive incentives that reinforce trends already underway in Indonesia.

Links to Rogue Groups and Muslim Extremists

Political fragmentation after the fall of Suharto encouraged the development of links between some active and retired senior military officers and rogue elements. Political stabilization and the development of healthy civil-military relations, as well as the requirements of military professionalism, will require the Indonesian political leadership and the TNI to take meaningful actions to break these links.

ELEMENTS OF A STRATEGY OF ENGAGEMENT WITH INDONESIA

Restoring IMET funding for Indonesia is the first priority. As noted in Chapter Eleven, because military training for Indonesia was effectively terminated in 1992, there has been a "lost generation" of Indonesian officers—officers who have no experience with the United States or who have no understanding of the importance that the United States military attaches to civilian leadership, democracy, and respect for human rights. U.S.–trained senior officers formed the core of the reformist wing of the TNI that sought to implement reforms after the downfall of President Suharto. As many of those officers retired, the impetus behind the military reform movement diminished. Therefore, rebuilding this core of U.S.–trained officers is a critical need, although, realistically, it will take years to undo the

---

[1]Another problem, according to former Minister of Defense Juwono Sudarsono, is the disconnect between the central headquarters and the units on the field. Individual commanders, especially in hardship areas, are dependent on local interests for financial and other support and are therefore beholden to those interests. The TNI headquarters has control over promotions and assignments, but not over the day-to-day behavior of the troops (interview with Juwono Sudarsono, Jakarta, February 2002).

damage done by the decade-long suspension of the IMET program for Indonesia.

An initial IMET package for Indonesia could include military medical training (for instance, trauma skills courses for troops engaged in field operations); safety training for the air force and navy; legal training—especially in rules of engagement and discipline problems—which is currently a priority along with counterterrorism training in Indonesian army training; and, of course, higher military education.

Another part of this engagement strategy would be to provide the assistance needed to prevent the further deterioration of Indonesian military capabilities, particularly in the area of air transport. An Indonesia that does not have the ability to defend itself or to respond on a timely basis to outbreaks of communal conflict is less likely to develop as a stable democracy. The current proposal to assist Indonesia with training and equipping a peacemaking unit with the capability of rapid deployment to areas of conflict would contribute greatly to the reestablishment of a climate of peace and security, without which political and economic reform cannot move forward. The United States should also extend support to the Jala Mangkara detachment (manned by both marine and navy personnel) and to the navy's Kopaska unit. Both of these units have the ability to conduct maritime counterterrorist operations and could play a role in interdicting illegal weapons shipments to Aceh and the Moluccas. Neither unit has been implicated in human rights violations.

Combined military exercises also provide valuable training opportunities. Indonesian military personnel should be invited to participate in the next multilateral Cobra Gold exercise (with the United States, Thailand, and Singapore). Indonesian counterterrorist and special forces should also be encouraged to participate in training exchanges with Philippine military units, such as the Scout Rangers, who have already been exposed to U.S. training.

Even if domestic politics in Indonesia make accountability for the use of U.S. equipment and training difficult to address to the satisfaction of the U.S. Congress, the United States can achieve important counterterrorism objectives by providing training and technical support for Indonesia's civilian National Intelligence Agency (BIN) and the military intelligence organization (BAIS). The focus of the assistance program could be on improving technical data collection and analytical capabilities. The program has other key benefits:

- First, it will present an opportunity to improve Indonesia's civilian and police intelligence organizations with new, specialized training and equipment. This will better enable those organizations to seek out and to apprehend international terrorists seeking shelter within Indonesian militant organizations.

- Second, the program will give the United States an opportunity to assist in the professionalization of the Indonesian intelligence community, which has been criticized for its human rights abuses and inappropriate covert operations. BAIS officials have indicated that they were interested in learning more about U.S. intelligence philosophy and increasing contacts with their U.S. counterparts.[2] The United States should take advantage of this window of opportunity to shape the thinking of this important sector of the Indonesian military establishment.

- Third, the program will assist Indonesia in reining in its domestic religious extremist organizations, which are allegedly linked to international terrorist groups and which have contributed so greatly to domestic instability and violence. The Indonesian military and intelligence services recognize the problem of external funding of extremist Islamic organizations in Indonesia, but have limited means to control the flow of funds. The United States should help the Indonesian government to develop the technical means to monitor and control these financial flows. The Indonesian government, for its own part, should secure the passage of adequate legislation to permit its security services to carry out their responsibilities in this area.

Finally, a word of caution: Despite the potential importance of U.S. engagement with Indonesia, the United States' ability to shape Indonesian military behavior and to hedge against adverse outcomes is limited. With some exceptions, notably air transport, the Indonesian military does not rely on high-technology equipment and is not dependent on the United States for its equipment and training.

---

[2]Angel Rabasa's discussion with BAIS officials, Jakarta, February 2002.

Also, there are limits to the ability of the United States to control how the equipment provided to Indonesia is used. Moreover, given the Indonesians' sensitivity to issues of sovereignty, there is a large potential downside to excessively intrusive behavior by an external power. These factors can complicate the task of developing a constructive cooperative relationship between the U.S. and Indonesian governments and militaries, but do not reduce the importance of that relationship.

CAN INDONESIA MEET THE LEAHY AMENDMENT CONDITIONS?

As we discussed in Chapter Eleven, the Leahy amendment (part of the FY2000 Foreign Operations appropriations and which was extended and expanded in the FY2001 and FY2002 legislation) banned military assistance to Indonesia. The amendment requires the U.S. president to certify to Congress that Indonesia has made progress in addressing specific actions related to human rights, accountability for the violence in East Timor after the independence referendum, and transparency in the Indonesian military budget before IMET funding and financing of military sales can be resumed.

Objective observers believe that progress has been made on all of the Leahy Amendment requirements except for accountability for misdeeds in East Timor. The new regional commander in West Timor (who is an ethnic Timorese from West Timor) has aggressively curtailed the activities of pro-Indonesia militia forces in West Timor and successfully disarmed most of them. Security has returned to the border between Indonesia and East Timor. Cross-border incursions into East Timor by militia patrols have been curtailed and there have been virtually no clashes with United Nations peacekeeping forces since mid-2001. More than 200,000 refugees have returned to East Timor. Most of the refugees who are remaining in West Timor are members of families with close connections to the Indonesian government or who are fearful of retaliation should they return to their homeland. On the matter of the killing of three United Nations workers on West Timor, the Indonesian court system—on government appeal—obtained far more severe sentences for the killers than had originally been prescribed.

The issue of accountability for alleged crimes has been a contentious problem for the TNI for many years. During the Suharto era, the TNI generally operated with impunity in its military operations against separatists and political activists. Some misdeeds by soldiers and junior officers were punished within the military and with little publicity, but senior commanders were almost never called on to account for the actions of the men under their command.

In the post-Suharto era, the army has introduced human rights instruction in all echelons of its training and education system, and has used agencies such as the International Committee of the Red Cross to present instruction to its officer corps. But despite the TNI's pledge to enforce proper human rights practices, and the addition of human rights training, there are persistent complaints about the conduct of the troops in field operations in which supervision and control of troops are notoriously weak. Following the most noteworthy incident of military misconduct since 1991, more than a dozen junior soldiers were convicted by court-martial for murdering civilians in Aceh, but the immediate commander of that operation disappeared and was never prosecuted. His whereabouts are still unknown.

This background is important for establishing the TNI mind-set on senior officer accountability. For colonels or officers of higher ranks to be punished for the misconduct of subordinates in East Timor—if those implicated did in fact order that misconduct—will require a significant change to a decades-long system of beliefs and actions that largely grants immunity to military personnel for their actions in the course of tactical operations.

Indonesia's own judicial system has identified 19 suspects implicated in five major atrocities in East Timor, and an ad hoc tribunal was formed specifically to hear those cases. The results of that effort—which were as yet unknown as of the time of this writing—will have a significant impact on the future of U.S.–Indonesian military-to-military relations.

Advocates of closer U.S.–Indonesian relations expect that punishment for some senior officers in the chain of command accused of ordering violent acts to be committed, as well as the junior officers who actually committed those violent acts, will help to bring about a compromise that would allow most forms of bilateral military cooperation to resume. On the other hand, a perceived whitewash will likely anger human rights advocates in NGOs and in the U.S. Congress, who could be expected to resist the easing of restrictions on U.S. military assistance to Indonesia.

BIBLIOGRAPHY

BOOKS

Baker, Richard W., et al., eds., *Indonesia: the Challenge of Change*, Institute of Southeast Asian Studies, Singapore, New York: St. Martin's Press, 1999.

Bresnan, John, *Managing Indonesia*, New York: Columbia University Press, 1993.

Brown, David, *State and Ethnic Politics in Southeast Asia*, London: Routledge, 1994.

Cribb, Robert, and Colin Brown, *Modern Indonesia: A History Since 1945*, London and New York: Longman, 1995.

Crouch, Harold, *The Army and Politics in Indonesia*, Ithaca, N.Y., and London: Cornell University Press, 1993.

Crouch, Harold, "Wiranto and Habibie: Military-Civilian Relations Since May 1998," in Arief Budiman, Barbara Hatley, and Damien Kingsbury, eds., *Reformasi: Crisis and Change in Indonesia*, Monash Asia Institute, Australia, 1999.

Crouch, Harold, "The TNI and East Timor Policy," in James J. Fox and Dionisio Babo Soares, eds., *Out of the Ashes: The Destruction and Reconstruction of East Timor*, Adelaide, Australia: Crawford Press, 2000.

Djalal, Dino Patti, *The Geopolitics of Indonesia's Maritime Territorial Policy,* Centre for Strategic and International Studies, Jakarta, 1996.

Fox, James J., and Dionisio Babo Soares, eds., *Out of the Ashes: The Destruction and Reconstruction of East Timor,* Adelaide, Australia: Crawford Press, 2000.

Han, Sung-Joo, *Changing Values in Asia: Their Impact on Governance and Development,* Japan Center for International Exchange and Institute of Southeast Asian Studies, Singapore, 1999.

Haseman, John, "The Misuse of Military Power and Misplaced Military Pride," in James J. Fox and Dionisio Babo Soares, eds., *Out of the Ashes: The Destruction and Reconstruction of East Timor,* Adelaide, Australia: Crawford Press, 2000.

Human Rights Watch, *Violence and Political Impasse in Papua,* New York, July 2001a.

Human Rights Watch, *Indonesia: The War in Aceh,* New York, August 2001b.

Indorf, Hans, *Impediments to Regionalism in Southeast Asia,* Institute for Southeast Asian Studies, Singapore, 1984.

International Institute for Strategic Studies, *The Military Balance, 2001/2002,* Oxford, U.K.: Oxford University Press, 2002.

Isaacson, Jason, and Colin Rubenstein, eds., *Islam in Asia: Changing Political Realities,* Washington, D.C., and Melbourne: American Jewish Committee and Australia/Israel and Jewish Affairs Committee, 1999.

Jane's World Air Forces, Jane's Information Group, 2001.

Jenkins, David, *Suharto and His Generals: Indonesian Military Politics 1975–1983,* Modern Indonesia Project, Ithaca, N.Y.: Cornell University, 1984.

Kammen, Douglas, and Siddharth Chandra, *A Tour of Duty: Changing Patterns of Military Politics in Indonesia in the 1990s,* Cornell Modern Indonesia Project, Ithaca, N.Y.: Cornell University, 1999.

Knowles, James, Ernesto Pernia, and Mary Racelis, *Social Consequences of the Financial Crisis in Asia,* Asian Development Bank, Manila, July 1999.

Kristiadi, J., "The Armed Forces," in Richard W. Baker, et al., eds., *Indonesia: the Challenge of Change,* Institute of Southeast Asian Studies, Singapore, New York: St. Martin's Press, 1999.

Liddle, R. William, *Leadership and Culture in Indonesian Politics,* Sydney, Australia: Allen and Unwin, 1996.

Lowry, Robert, *The Armed Forces of Indonesia,* St. Leonards, Australia: Allen & Unwin, 1996.

McDonald, Hamish, *Suharto's Indonesia,* Sydney, Australia: Fontana, 1980.

Morrison, Charles E., ed., *Asia Pacific Security Outlook 1999,* ASEAN Institute for Strategic and International Studies, East-West Center, and Japan Center for International Exchange, Tokyo and New York, 1999.

Mulvenon, James, *Soldiers of Fortune: The Rise and Fall of the Chinese Military-Business Complex, 1978–1998,* Armonk, N.Y., and London: M.E. Sharpe, 2001.

Nasution, A. H., *Memenuhi Panggilan Tugas,* Jakarta: CV Haji Masagung, 1985.

Noer, John H., *Chokepoints: Maritime Economic Concerns in Southeast Asia,* Washington, D.C.: National Defense University, 1996.

PPW-LIPI Research Team (Tim Peneliti PPW-LIPI), *Tentara Mendamba Mitra,* Bandung, Indonesia: Mizan, 1999.

Rabasa, Angel, and Peter Chalk, *Indonesia's Transformation and Its Implications for Regional Stability,* Santa Monica, Calif.: RAND, MR-1344-AF, 2001.

Samego, Indria, et al., *Bila ABRI Berbisnis,* Bandung, Indonesia: Mizan, 1998a.

Samego, Indria, et al., *Bila ABRI Menghendaki: Desakan-Kuat Reformasi Atas Konsep Dwifungsi ABRI,* Bandung, Indonesia: Mizan, 1998b.

Schwarz, Adam, *A Nation in Waiting: Indonesia in the 1990s,* Boulder, Colo.: Westview, 1994.

Singh, Bilveer, *ABRI and the Security of Southeast Asia,* Singapore Institute of International Affairs, Singapore, 1994.

Soedjati, Djiwandono, and Yong Mun Cheong, eds., *Soldiers and Stability in Southeast Asia,* Institute of Southeast Asian Studies, Singapore, 1988.

Sokolsky, Richard, Angel Rabasa, and C. Richard Neu, *The Role of Southeast Asia in U.S. Strategy Toward China,* Santa Monica, Calif.: RAND, MR-1170-AF, 2000.

Sundhaussen, Ulf, *The Road to Power: Indonesian Military Politics, 1945–1967,* Oxford, U.K., and Kuala Lumpur: Oxford University Press, 1982.

Tjokropranolo, *General Sudirman: The Leader Who Finally Destroyed Colonialism in Indonesia,* Australian Defence Studies Centre, Canberra, 1995.

Vatikiotis, Michael, *Indonesian Politics Under Suharto: Order and Pressure for Change,* London: Routledge, 1993.

Woodward, Mark R., ed., *Toward a New Paradigm: Recent Developments in Indonesian Islamic Thought,* Tempe, Ariz.: Arizona State University Press, 1996.

Wurfel, David, and Bruce Burton, eds., *Southeast Asia in the New World Order,* New York: St. Martin's Press, 1996

Yayasan Insan Politika Research Team (Tim Peneliti Yayasan Insan Politika), *Tentara Yang Gelisah,* Bandung, Indonesia: Mizan, 1999.

MONOGRAPHS, ARTICLES, AND PAPERS

"1,850 Troops Set for Aceh," The *Jakarta Post*, April 1, 2002.

George Aditjondro, "Financing Human Rights Violations in Indonesia," *Indonesia ALERT!* January 2001, www.indonesiaalert.org/index.html.

Alhadar, Smith, "The Forgotten War in North Maluku," *Inside Indonesia*, No. 63, July–September 2000.

"Army Chief Lashes Out at Bickering Politicians," *The Jakarta Post*, November 17, 2000.

"Army Wants to Crush Rebels as Police Fail," *Indonesia–News IO*, December 15, 2000.

"Bimantoro's Insubordination Lauded by Some," *The Jakarta Post*, July 8, 2001.

Bjornlund, Eric, "Supporting the Democratic Transition Process in Indonesia," statement before the U.S. House of Representatives, Committee on International Relations, Subcommittee on Asia and the Pacific, Washington, D.C., February 16, 2000.

Callahan, Mary P., "Civil-Military Relations in Indonesia: Reformasi and Beyond," Occasional Paper No. 4, The Center for Civil-Military Relations, Naval Postgraduate School, Monterey, Calif., September 1999.

Clad, James, "Security in Southeast Asia," in William M. Carpenter and David G. Wiencek, eds., *Asian Security Handbook 2000*, New York and London: M.E. Sharpe, 2000.

"The Conflict in Central Sulawesi," Building Human Security in Indonesia, Program on Humanitarian Policy and Conflict Research, The President and Fellows of Harvard College, 2001, www.preventconflict.org/portal/main/maps_sulawesi_conflict.php.

"Current Data on the Indonesian Military Elite," *Indonesia*, Cornell University, Ithaca, New York, No. 71, April 2001.

"Cutting Closer to the Bone," *Far Eastern Economic Review*, May 24, 2001.

"Djoko Vows to End Maluku's Military-Police Conflict," *The Jakarta Post*, June 7, 2002.

Emmerson, Donald, "Indonesia's Eleventh Hour in Aceh," *PacNet 49*, December 17, 1999.

Erawan, Ketut Putra, "Political Reform and Regional Politics in Indonesia," *Asian Survey*, Vol. 39, No. 4, 1999.

Espinosa, Juan Carlos, and Robert C. Harding II, "Olive Green Parachutes and Slow Motion Piñatas: The Cuban Armed Forces in the Economy and in Transition," *Problems of Post-Communism*, Vol. 48, No. 6, November–December 2001.

"ExxonMobil, in Fear, Exits Indonesian Gas Fields," *The New York Times*, March 24, 2001.

"ExxonMobil Rides Out Squalls in Indonesia," *Far Eastern Economic Review*, August 16, 2001.

Federation of American Scientists, "Intelligence Resource Program: Free Aceh Movement," www.fas.org/irp/world/para/aceh.htm (last updated September 13, 1999).

"The Genesis of the Indonesian National Army and Some Political Implications," http://kb.nl.infolev/inginfo/fondscat/toelicht/nib/purbo.html, (n.d.).

"Gotong Royong Cabinet Ministers," Embassy of the Republic of Indonesia, Ottawa, Canada, August 9, 2001, www.indonesia-ottawa.org/Government/Cabinets/chris-dagg.htm.

Habib, A. Hasnan, "The Future of the Indonesian Armed Forces," paper presented at the CSCAP Seminar on Indonesia's Future Challenges and Implications for the Region, Jakarta, March 8, 2000.

"Hamzah Demands U.S. Stop Attack on Afghan," *The Jakarta Post*, October 15, 2001.

Haseman, John B., "The United States, IMET, and Indonesia," *U.S.–Indonesia Society Report*, No. 3, January 1998.

Haseman, John B., "Indonesia Plans 'Intel' Reorganization," *Jane's Intelligence Review*, December 1, 2000.

Haseman, John B., "Realistic Military Reform Prospects in Indonesia," *Van Zorge Report*, Vol. 3, No. 6, April 2001.

Human Rights Watch, "Indonesia: Why Aceh Is Exploding," New York, August 27, 1999, www.igc.org/hrw/campaigns/indonesia/aceh0827.htm.

"Indonesia's Military Power Play," *Asia Times*, December 1, 2001.

Ingo W., "Indonesia's New Intelligence Agency. How? Why? and What For?" *Watch Indonesia*, No. 1, Nov. 1, 2000, http://home.snafu.de/watchin/BIN.html.

International Crisis Group, "Indonesia's Crisis: Chronic but Not Acute," ICG Indonesia Report No. 2, Jakarta and Brussels, May 31, 2000a.

International Crisis Group, "Indonesia: Keeping the Military Under Control," ICG Asia Report No. 9, Jakarta and Brussels, September 5, 2000b.

International Crisis Group, "Indonesia: Police Reform," ICG Asia Report No. 13, Jakarta and Brussels, February 20, 2001a.

International Crisis Group, "Aceh: Why Military Force Won't Bring Lasting Peace," ICG Asia Report No. 17, Jakarta and Brussels, June 12, 2001b.

International Crisis Group, "Indonesia: Ending Repression in Irian Jaya," ICG Asia Report No. 23, Jakarta and Brussels, September 20, 2001c.

International Crisis Group, "Indonesia: Next Steps in Military Reform," Asia Report No. 24, Jakarta and Brussels, October 11, 2001d.

International Crisis Group, "Indonesia: The Search for Peace in Maluku," ICG Asia Report No. 31, Jakarta and Brussels, February 8, 2002.

"International Peacekeepers Pour into East Timor," *The New York Times*, September 21, 1999.

"Invisible Commander, Invisible Troops," *Tempo*, April 2–8, 2002.

"Is There an Al-Qaeda Connection in Indonesia?" *Sunday Straits Times*, Singapore, January 20, 2002.

Jackson, Karl, "The Military in Indonesian Politics," mimeo, April 26, 1998.

"Jakarta Arrests Leaders of Separatist Movement in Easternmost Province," *Wall Street Journal*, November 30, 2000.

Johanson, Vanessa, "The Sultan Will Be Dr Hasan Tiro," *Inside Indonesia*, No. 60, 1999.

"Kaster TNI Letjen Agus Widjoyo: TNI Tak Ingin Lagi Tangani Fungsi Teritorial," *Kompas*, August 22, 2001.

"Kiki Syahnakri: A Real Officer and a Gentleman," *The Jakarta Post*, May 14, 2002.

Kingsbury, Damien, "The Reform of the Indonesian Armed Forces," *Contemporary Southeast Asia*, Vol. 22, No. 2, August 2000.

Koekebakker, Welmoed, "Cracks in the Cilangkap Bastion: The Armed Forces in Suharto's Indonesia," Amsterdam: ENAAT Publications, July 24, 1994, www.antenna.nl/enaat/indones.html.

"KPN Reports Findings in Theys' Alleged Murder Case," *The Jakarta Post*, March 26, 2002.

Kyrway, Idris, "Analysis of the Political Situation in Indonesia," Kyrway Report 2000-6, Support for Decentralization Measures, October 2000.

"Looking for SE Asia's Own Carlos the Jackal," *The Jakarta Post*, January 30, 2002.

MacFarling, Ian, *The Dual Function of the Indonesian Armed Forces: Military Politics in Indonesia*, Australian Defence Studies Centre, University of New South Wales, Sydney, 1996.

MacFarling, Ian, "Some Thoughts on the Indonesian Armed Forces," briefing, conference, Arlington, Va., April 20, 2001.

"Maluku: The Conflict," Building Human Security in Indonesia, Program on Humanitarian Policy and Conflict Research, The President and Fellows of Harvard College, 2001, www. preventconflict.org/portal/main/maps_maluku_conflict.php.

McCulloch, Lesley, "Trifungsi: The Role of the Indonesian Military in Business," The International Conference on Soldiers in Business: Military as an Economic Actor, Bonn International Center for Conversion, Jakarta, October 17–19, 2000.

McCulloch, Lesley, "Power and Money Drive Aceh Military Solution," The Jakarta Post, January 30, 2002.

"Military Professionalism Pays Off, but Not Enough to End Conflict in Aceh," The Jakarta Post, April 15, 2002.

"MPR Team Agrees to Hold Snap Session If Necessary," The Jakarta Post, July 9, 2001.

National Democratic Institute, "The Beginning of Stability? Indonesia's Change of President and Government," Washington, D.C., July/August 2001.

Noer, Rosita S., "The Military Role in Indonesia: The Ups and Downs of Military Involvement in Indonesian Politics," unpublished manuscript, 2000.

"Osama bin Laden and Indonesia," Laksamana.net, Jakarta, September 12, 2001, http://laksamana.net/vnews.cfm?ncat=19&&news_id+1175.

Pereira, Derwin, "Why Things Fell Apart: Unrest in Indonesia," The Straits Times, Singapore, December 20, 1998.

Pereira, Derwin, "Musical Chairs in Indonesia," The Straits Times, Singapore, January 17, 1999.

Pereira, Derwin, "Joget with the Generals," The Straits Times, Singapore, September 24, 2000.

Pereira, Derwin, "Is There an Al-Qaeda Connection in Indonesia?" *Sunday Straits Times*, Singapore, January 20, 2002.

Peters, Ralph, "Also Known as Indonesia: Notes on the Javanese Empire," unpublished paper, 2002.

"The Puppet President," *FEER*, August 2, 2001.

"Red Beret Business," *Tempo*, April 16, 2002.

Severino, Rodolfo C., "Indonesia and the Future of ASEAN," paper presented at the CSCAP Seminar on Indonesia's Future Challenges and Implications for the Region, Jakarta, March 9, 2000.

Shiraishi, Takashi, "The Indonesian Military in Politics," unpublished mimeo, 1998.

Sidwell, Thomas E., "The Indonesian Military: Dwi Fungsi and Territorial Operations," Foreign Military Studies Office, Ft. Leavenworth, Kan., 1995.

Singh, Bilveer, "The Indonesian Military Business Complex: Origins, Course and Future," Strategic & Defence Studies Centre Working Paper No. 354, Australian National University, Canberra, 2001.

Smith, Anthony L., "Indonesia's Role in ASEAN: The End of Leadership?" *Contemporary Southeast Asia*, Vol. 21, No. 2, August 1999.

Smith, Anthony L., "Indonesia's Foreign Policy Under Abdurrahman Wahid: Radical or Status Quo State?" *Contemporary Southeast Asia*, Vol. 22, No. 3, December 2000.

"Squeezed by the Logging Business," *Tempo*, April 2–8, 2002.

"Special Report on Poso, Indonesia: A Crisis Narrowly Averted but Still Dangerous and Unstable," Reformed Ecumenical Council, Gospel Communications International, 2002, www.gospelcom. net/rec/Poso.html.

"Sulawesi: Actors," Building Human Security in Indonesia, Program on Humanitarian Policy and Conflict Research, The President and Fellows of Harvard College, 2001, www.preventconflict.org/ portal/main/maps_sulawesi_actors.php.

"Swedish-Based GAM: Talk or Fight—Not Both," *The Jakarta Post*, January 31, 2002.

Syafruddin, Ayip, "Why Laskar Jihad Is Heading to Poso?" Central Board of Ahlus Sunnah wal Jama'ah Communication Forum, Yogyakarta, Indonesia, 2000, www.laskarjihad.or.id/english/article/headingtoposo.htm.

Tan Sri Zainal Abidin Sulong, "The Regional Impact and the Role of the Region in Indonesia's Transformation," paper presented at the CSCAP Seminar on Indonesia's Future Challenges and Implications for the Region, Jakarta, March 9, 2000.

Tapol, "Hendropriyono and Bambang Kesowo, The Key Figures in Megawati's Kitchen Cabinet," The Indonesian Human Rights Campaign, Surrey, U.K., August 21, 2001, www.gn.apc.org/tapol/st010821.htm.

"Terjadi Pembangkangan Militer Atas Kepemimpinan Sipil," *Kompas*, December 6, 2001.

"Territorial Shift 'Needs Time,'" *The Thompson & Thompson Report*, Jakarta, October 16, 2001.

"TNI Accused of 'Hidden Martial Law' in Malukus," *Straits Times* Singapore, May 30, 2002.

"TNI to Downgrade Territorial Affairs Post," *The Jakarta Post*, October 30, 2001.

"TNI to Study Territorial Function," *The Jakarta Post*, March 3, 2000.

United States-Indonesia Society, "Parliamentary Elections in Indonesia," Washington, D.C., June 22, 1999.

U.S. Committee for Refugees, "Political History of Aceh," September 9, 1999, www.refugees.org/news/crisis/indonesia/aceh.htm.

Van Langenberg, Michael, "End of the Jakartan Empire?" *Inside Indonesia*, No. 61, January–March 2000.

The White House, Office of the Press Secretary, "Joint Statement Between the United States of America and the Republic of Indonesia," Washington, D.C., September 19, 2001.

NEWSPAPERS AND PERIODICALS

Asia Times (Hong Kong)

Asiaweek

The Bulletin of Indonesian Economic Studies

Contemporary Southeast Asia (ISEAS Singapore)

The Economist

The Far Eastern Economic Review

The Indonesian Observer (Jakarta)

The Indonesian Quarterly (Jakarta)

The Jakarta Post

Kompas (Jakarta)

Kyrway Report (Jakarta)

PacNet Newsletter, Center for Strategic and International Studies, Washington, D.C.

The Straits Times (Singapore)

Tempo (Jakarta)

Van Zorge Report on Indonesia (Jakarta)

The Wall Street Journal

Weekly Update, International Republican Institute, Washington, D.C.

CONFERENCES

Asia Society, Sasakawa Peace Foundation USA, and United States–Indonesia Society, "Communities in Conflict and Implications for U.S.–Indonesian Relations," Washington, D.C., June 18, 2002.

United States–Indonesia Society, "Indonesia's Military: Backbone of the Nation or Achilles' Heel?" proceedings of USINDO Workshop, Washington, D.C., March 28, 2000.

United States–Indonesia Society, "Indonesia Today: Current Trends, Future Possibilities," report of USINDO Workshop, Washington, D.C., March 13, 2001.

United States–Indonesia Society, open forum with Michael Vatikiotis, editor, *Far Eastern Economic Review*, Washington, D.C., January 30, 2002.

United States–Indonesia Society, open forum on "Indonesia's Changing Security Structure," with Lieutenant General Agus Widjojo and Colonel (retired) John Haseman, Washington, D.C., February 21, 2002.

United States–Indonesia Society, open forum with Ahmad Ma'arif, chairman, Muhammadiyah, and Dr. Jusuf Wanandi, chairman, Jakarta Center for Strategic and International Studies, Washington, D.C., April 8, 2002.

Angel Rabasa (Ph.D., Harvard University) is a senior policy analyst with the RAND Corporation, specializing in regional security affairs. He is the author of numerous books and articles on Southeast Asian security. His most recent RAND publication, with Peter Chalk, is *Indonesia's Transformation and the Stability of Southeast Asia* (2001). Before joining RAND, Dr. Rabasa served in U.S. Departments of State and Defense positions overseas and in Washington, D.C.

Colonel John B. Haseman, U.S. Army (retired), is one of the United States' leading experts on the Indonesian military. Colonel Haseman served for ten years between 1978 and 1994 in assignments to the U.S. Embassy in Jakarta. His last assignment there was as U.S. Defense and Army Attache from 1990 to 1994. Colonel Haseman has written and consulted widely in Indonesian defense and political-military affairs.